John Lyons' The Making of a Perfect Horse

Private Lessons

John Lyons Answers Your Questions on Care and Training

ISBN: 1-879-620-63-4

Belvoir Publications Inc.
Box 2626
75 Holly Hill Lane
Greenwich, CT 06836 USA

Lyons. John
Private Lessons: John Lyons Answers Your Questions
                    on Care and Training
Lyons, John
and the editors of John Lyons' Perfect Horse

ISBN: 1-879-620-63-4
1. Horses - Training   2. Horsemanship   3. Horses

Manufactured in the United States of America

John Lyons' The Making of a Perfect Horse

Private Lessons

John Lyons Answers Your Questions on Care and Training

John Lyons
and the editors of John Lyons' Perfect Horse

Belvoir Publications, Inc.
Greenwich, CT

Contents

Section III: Putting Theory into Practice

Note: Throughout this book, we use some terms and refer to
some lessons that may be familiar to those who are students of
John's methods or have read the other books in this series. If they
are new to you, however, our "Helpful Info" section on page 203
should help make them more understandable.

Preface

Good coaching involves two major things — teaching good technique and encouraging someone to put that technique into practice. This book is mostly about the last part — helping you realize that you (yes, you!) can build a great relationship with your horse and that you can safely control his behavior. The messages in my editorials, as well as the success stories of other horse owners, are meant to cheer you on when you are downhearted or unsure about what to do next in your horse's training. I know what it's like to feel discouraged. But I also know that reminding ourselves of what we can do, and what others have successfully done, will lift us up.

You don't have to have a special gift to work with horses — any thinking, caring person can do it. As I've gone around the country the last 20-plus years, if there's one thing that has really impressed me, it's how caring horsepeople are. Who else would come home from a long day of work to muck stalls and wash water buckets? Or stay up all night to keep an eye on a colicky horse? Or to help another horseperson? Who is in a better position to encourage us but our fellow horsepeople?

This book contains lots of advice — my philosophy of training, answers to riders' questions, Dr. Eleanor Kellon's answers to questions about vet care, and advice from the readers of *John Lyons' Perfect Horse* magazine — but it also contains lots of encouragement. May God richly bless you and your family as you work with your perfect horses.

May the Lord bless you and protect you.
May the Lord smile on you and be gracious to you. May the Lord show you his favor and give you his peace.
                    Numbers 6:24-26

Section I

John's Editorials

1

Trusting Your Instincts

Does it seem like horse problems are difficult to solve? Do you wish there was a magic formula to follow? Don't feel bad; everybody does. There's no quick answer, but frequently I'm able to help folks solve a problem just by asking a series of questions. They actually knew the answers all along but hadn't developed an effective line of thinking or they were afraid they would make a mistake.

Just as you set the horse up so he'll discover the right answer, in my training principles we try to set you up so you'll discover the solution to the riding or training problems you have. No one can hand you a recipe that will cover every situation. Success with horse training involves focusing on what you want the horse to do, determining what you can do with him now, and developing a way to take him from Point A to Point B.

There are some rules we go by so we know when we are on the right track, and then we put as many steps in the lesson plan as we can. That way, if the horse has a problem at one step, we can backtrack to the step he did perfectly.

It's my belief that God considers the horse to be valuable, a very special animal. Now, would you give something you thought valuable to someone who wouldn't take care of it? I doubt it. I don't believe God has done that, either. When God gave us horses, I believe he also gave us a sense of what is right and wrong to do with them. We may not always know how to train them, but if we are doing something that will hurt them, or if someone else offers to do something that's not good, our instincts will almost always tell us.

I've heard many stories from owners who admit they suspected that what their trainer was doing was wrong or hurtful to the horse, but because he was the trainer, they deferred to his experience. If you own a horse, the responsibility to take care of him is yours, and that includes making sure that others don't mistreat him in the name of "training."

I like to say that we teach our horses, rather than train them. What passes as "horse training" is different from what we accept as "education," but it shouldn't be. Horses don't deliberately disobey us. If they know the right answer, they'll give it to us, because they know it will be better for them in the end.

Your instincts to care for your horse come from someone who also cares for your horse — God. As much as he cares for your horse, however, He cares even more for you. So use your instincts to make choices that are good for both you and your perfect horse. ▣

2

"Control" Is A Good Word

When we hear the word "control," we often bristle, as if control were a bad thing. Handled properly, it's really a good thing; and trust and respect, other good things, are actually byproducts of it. We know we want our horses under control, but we also want their trust and respect.

This is the equation: Control without pain produces trust and respect. Trust and respect are the foundation for a relationship.

Let's look at how that works in a human situation. We don't mind someone controlling our time, for instance, if it is done fairly and in kindness. When our boss determines what time we come to work, what work we do and how much we get paid, that's control. If it's done wisely, our confidence in his leadership grows. That's respect. As we respect him, we continue to allow him to control our activity in that manner. Continued respect becomes trust. By the time we say that we trust someone, we have developed a good relationship with them.

But, without trust, even control is only temporary. If our boss exerts control in a rude manner, then respect is lost, trust is broken, and soon we're looking for a new boss.

Then, too, when we use self-control, our self-respect grows. Think how good you feel when you say "no" to a wrong activity, or when you refuse to lose your temper just because you are angry. You end up feeling a bigger person for exercising restraint. And, when we control our tongue, not saying an unkind thing just because we thought of it, we feel proud of ourselves. Our self-confidence grows, too.

When we control our horse's actions without causing him pain, his respect for us grows. But if we bully him, that respect takes the form of fear, as it would if we were being bullied. And while the horse may obey us momentarily, he's not voluntarily turning control over to us, so we're not developing trust. Trust comes when the horse realizes that he is being controlled painlessly.

So, if you are not controlling your horse — if you're trying to get him to like you with smooches and treats — you really don't have a trusting, respectful relationship. Horses live in a pecking-order world, and they respect and trust the horse who tells them where to eat and who helps them hold a standard of behavior. They don't resent control if it's done right — they are secure when they know their place. And we are only safe when our great big horse knows his place in our herd — below us. We can learn to think of control as a positive word, so we have better relationships with our perfect horses. **PH**

3

He Didn't Mean
To Hurt Me

ore people are hurt by horses who "love" them than by horses who have never been ridden. That's because people know to expect untrained-horse behavior from untrained horses. But, too often, we presume that because a horse has been ridden for years, he is trained.

Have you ever read an ad offering a "gentle" horse for sale? In most cases, that means the horse will follow you around the pasture. But put the same untrained horse under saddle, and the picture changes. Horses aren't naturally aggressive (unlike lions or tigers), so it's only natural that they follow the source of treats and petting. But, it's just as natural for them to try to get away when they feel threatened — and possibly hurt someone in the process.

When a horse acts naturally, he's not always safe to ride or to be around. Our horse has to be trained, his instinctive reactions replaced with conditioned responses, if we want him to be even a safe pet.

So why are people hurt by horses who "love" them? It's because we assume that horses are like people. If we care about someone, we do what we think is in that person's best interest. But a horse does what his instinct tells him or what he's been trained to do. Affection has nothing to do with his performance, and consequently, misbehavior should not be mistaken for betrayal.

Also, people assume that because a horse is a certain age, he has a certain base of training. If he hasn't been trained not to be head-shy, for instance, he's still what I would consider an "unbroke" horse and likely to get you hurt — regardless of how old he is.

Still another tendency, when we feel affection for a horse, is to excuse his bad behavior. We don't want to risk losing his affection. Or we may attribute poor manners to a prior bad experience we think the horse had. So when our horse puts his ears back as we go in his stall to feed him, we might wrongly assume that because he's normally smoochy, he won't bite us. Or maybe we even put up with a horse who won't stand tied, overlooking that behavior because he was abused as a young horse.

The fact is, how we think the horse feels about us doesn't keep us safe; how he's trained does. Don't excuse bad behavior. The kindest thing you can do is help your horse get over it. He won't quit liking you. In fact, he'll like you better the more you get him in the habit of obeying. There's no reason to get hurt — even by a loving perfect horse. ▣

4

Don't Get Locked Up

As I go around the country, I see the same thing again and again. Horses out of control or on the verge of being out of control, and people who are afraid of doing the wrong thing. Somewhere along the way they've been told that training a horse is so complicated it has to be done by an expert. Some horses do require real expertise to get them started or re-started, but the average horse is being trained by his owner, whether the owner intends to train him or not.

So often horse people box themselves in. We do things the way we've done them in the past or seen them done and are afraid to try new methods, afraid to experiment to see what works and what doesn't. We have to be willing to adapt and learn from the horses and people around us.

Often someone will tell me about a problem. They'll say they have done "this and this" to solve it. I ask them if it's working. They tell me "no." I ask why they don't try something else. Their answer is they thought "this" was supposed to work, that it was the "right" way to do it. That mindset amazes me. We get stuck in the same way a horse might "lock up."

There is no one right way to do anything. We all learn as we go along. Because of the number of horses I work, I can tell you what usually works and what doesn't, but you have to adapt it to your own situation and abilities.

People who attend my symposiums year after year know that my training doesn't stay the same. I don't set out to make changes, but the more horses I work, the more I experiment and learn. I trained horses just fine years ago, and could train them just as well now using the same techniques, but as I continue to grow as a horseman, I find I've developed better and better ways of doing things. The principles that I train by haven't changed, but the techniques have.

Whatever you have been taught about horse training is probably more complicated than it needs to be. Remember the three rules of horse training: The trainer can't get hurt, the horse can't get hurt, and the horse should be calmer at the end of the lesson than he was at the beginning. Since your horse is made up of three parts — mental, emotional and physical — be sure that your training program takes all three into account. And develop a good relationship with your horse, communicating in ways meaningful to the horse and posing questions to which the horse can answer "yes." Don't be afraid to try something new. Don't let your pride or tradition keep you locked up in training methods that aren't working for you.

A Bible verse warns about not being imprisoned by philosophies that depend on human tradition and the principles of the world, rather than on Jesus Christ. It doesn't mean traditional ways are all bad; it means you shouldn't get enslaved by them. It's good advice about horse training, too. Don't be taken captive by training methods that depend on tradition or other people's opinions. Find out what works; look to what is true. God bless you as you progress with patience and confidence down the road with your perfect horse. ▣

5

Living In Today

We don't have to live in yesterday. We can live in today, like our horse does. One of the outstanding characteristics of the horse is his ability to forgive, to recognize when our behavior changes and to adapt to that new behavior.

But the horse has a tremendous memory. I was reminded of that recently. I roped a steer off Zip. Now, it had been at least six or seven years since I'd roped a calf or steer off him, yet he knew his job. I'd roped horses off him, so he had that experience recently, but calf roping is different. It requires him to face the calf and hold the line taut even after I've stepped off him. Although blind and out of practice, he remembered his job.

So, when we have a horse who was headshy and now isn't, or who was spooky, but now faces scary objects instead of

fleeing from them, we shouldn't think for a moment that the horse has forgotten about those experiences. He's just made adjustments. That's why it's so easy to train a horse. As we get consistent, the horse adapts, not holding against us what we may have done to him, however inadvertently, in the past. Even horses who have been abused by an owner change when the owner changes his or her behavior. It's as if the horse recognizes the change and forgives the offense.

I believe that the horse reflects much about his Creator, like a painting reflecting its artist. That ability to forgive and put past offenses behind them is undeniably something the horse and God have in common. I think it's something we're to have in common as well.

If we have a hard time forgiving someone of some offense, maybe it's because we're living too much in the past. Just like the horse, we may not automatically forget a hurtful experience, but we shouldn't have to live in it, either.

If a horse has a specific fear we are aware of, we have a responsibility to help him conquer it. If he is spooky — easily alarmed and tending to be out of control — then we should teach him how to handle scary experiences. Bad scares have long-reaching effects, but when we become consistent and show the horse that it's OK to be afraid (just as long as he doesn't run when he's scared), then the horse puts the past behind him.

When people or experiences change in our lives, we need to adapt and live in today. By doing so, we will reflect a little more of our Creator and also be a little more in tune with our perfect horse. ■PH■

6

One Thing At A Time

D o you know how horses are like most men but unlike most women? (Really, this is not a trick question.) Answer: They have one-track minds. When four men are, say, eating lunch together, one will be talking and three listening. In a group of four women, there may be three conversations going on, and all four women can tell you what any one said.

Likewise, many women can talk on the phone and do three other things at the same time without missing a beat. But, try to get a message to a man while he's on the phone. He has to interrupt his phone call to listen to what is being said in the room he's in.

Horses operate the same way as most men, focusing on just one thing at a time. (That's why he really didn't hear you when you talked to him while he was busy.)

Now, a smart rider can use this horse trait to his or her advantage. Can the horse be calling to his buddy while he's answering your

call to him on the rein? Obviously not. Most people's experience is that the horse focusing on his buddy ignores the rider. He may not be willfully ignoring the rider — he just has something else on his mind. So, our job is to replace his thoughts of the other horse with thoughts about our request.

That's why repetition is so important in teaching our horse to obey our cues. We want to bypass his thinking mechanism and condition him to respond to the cues automatically. That way, regardless of what else is going on in his life, when we use, for instance, the "calm down" cue, the horse will automatically drop his head and calm down. He won't have to make a conscious decision about it.

It's also why, when we use only one rein, the horse can understand a request for even complicated maneuvers. It works because he hears just one "voice" speaking to him at a time.

When we first teach any cue, the horse has to figure out what we are asking him to do. It takes a tremendous number of repetitions, consistently asking the same question the same way, and rewarding the same response, before the horse really understands what a specific cue means. From there, he'll go through learning cycles, one time seeming to know, another time not knowing what's being asked of him.

If the trainer gets frustrated at a low point in the cycle, and changes the request or fails to reward a correct response, the horse becomes confused, which makes the process take even longer.

The more we're able to present single requests to our horses, the faster they'll learn. No horse can really focus on more than one thing at a time — not even a perfect horse. **PH**

7

Your Horse Is "Your" Horse

We each have our reasons for involvement with horses. For some, it may be sport, others companionship, others prestige, nostalgia, peer pressure, physical exercise, the desire to reach personal goals, a method of enjoying nature, transportation to a campsite, the fun of trying to breed and raise great athletes, having something to love and care for and be loved by, or for others it may be just the lifestyle they've always lived. Some people can't even tell you why they love horses, which is OK because there's no "right" reason.

But knowing "why" can help determine training priorities. Some-

times a trainer naturally assumes goals for a horse, which may be different from the owner's. Unless this is discussed, tension can result. The owner may feel inadequate — that he'll never achieve the goals set by the trainer. He sometimes feels bad that his horse isn't as

fancy or well-bred as others in the barn. Worse yet, he may get pushed into activities beyond his ability or training — and injury to the horse or rider can result.

We've all known people who have been injured, for instance, by jumping a course too high for their level of training. Or we've heard of a horse laid up by injuries caused by a trainer pushing too hard, too fast, to get him to a big show. Trainers are often under pressure to produce, but in turn they sometimes create pressure for owners and horses where none needs to be.

If we, as trainers, presume that we know what's best for people and their horses, we do them a disservice. We should listen to the owner's goals and problems, before suggesting a route of training or even that their horse may be unsuitable for them.

This goes both ways. Owners have a responsibility to tell their trainers what they want from the training and from their horse. Then reasonable expectations can be set.

I remember a time when I was first doing clinics. I offered to pick up a horse that the owner couldn't load into the trailer. After working with the horse and outlining all that we could teach the horse, the owner asked me if she had to ride the horse. That made me stop and think. I had presumed that her goal was to have a riding horse, but she just wanted a pet to love and care for. It was her outlet for stress, and she didn't want to add stress to her life by riding. That changed the whole picture.

As a horse owner, be sure that you are the one setting expectations for yourself and your horse. Don't get pressured into meeting someone else's standards. Your horse isn't someone else's; he's your horse — your perfect horse. **PH**

8

You Cooped Him Up ...

H ave you ever considered the fact that, in the wild, the horse is a self-reliant animal? He finds his own food and water, rolls in the dust when he needs a bath, finds a buddy to scratch his withers if he has an itch — he doesn't need humans in his life, not at all.

But as soon as we put a corral around him, he loses that ability to fend for himself — which means we have to assume responsibility for his care. That involves more than just throwing him hay and topping off his water trough.

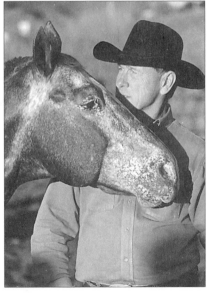

When we take a horse home and ask him to live in a stall, separated from other horses, it's an unnatural environment. It's up to us to provide for his social needs — whether that means turnout with other horses, making sure he can at least see other animals from his stall or spending time with him ourselves. Some behavior problems, like biting, can be the result of a horse not having balanced social interaction. The more time the horse spends away from other horses, the greater is our responsibility to interact with him correctly.

We all know about keeping the horse's hooves properly trimmed or shod. Can you imagine what it would be like to outgrow your shoes but have to wear them anyway? Or to have to go barefoot on just one foot?

And since the horse can't roam a vast terrain leaving parasites behind him as he goes, he sheds parasites into his own pasture or stall. Keeping him current on deworming isn't optional.

When we do chores, such as feeding or cleaning the barn, we should realize that those things have real importance. They are not just part of our schedule — they are part of our moral obligation.

More than just a responsibility, it's a God-given privilege. When God asked Adam to name the animals, that was a way of telling Adam that God was giving him the use of the animals, but with the responsibility to care for them.

So next time you are tempted to short-change your faithful buddy — failing to clean his water bucket, assuming his shoeing can wait a few weeks, assuming that a saddle-fit problem is a behavior problem or just skimping on stall bedding — remember he can't fend for himself. Remember your responsibility to your perfect horse. **PH**

9

How Many Horses?

How many horses can you take care of? I don't mean how many can you afford to feed, but how many can you actually care for? Care means more than just feeding our horses or arranging for their shoeing. It means having enough time to be sure that each horse is comfortable — that he gets hosed off if he's hot and sweaty or blanketed if he's likely to get cold. It means making sure that he gets the right kind of exercise and at appropriate intervals. And certainly it means making sure that he always stands in a clean stall or pasture. But we all know this. Right?

We may know it instinctively, but the pressures and desires of life often force us to act otherwise. It may happen without our even being aware of it, facilitated by the size of our barn or pastures. Who can resist adding one more horse? If we have an open stall, we're going to fill it,

whether with a horse of special breeding or a rescue case. We often just get by; but then, when our horses have extra needs, we don't have the time available to help them.

No matter how many shortcuts we learn, horses require time. The more horses we have, the less time we end up taking with each one. We find ourselves cutting corners cleaning stalls, washing water buckets or grooming. Before long, if we have too many horses, not only are we not caring for them as well as we'd like, we don't have time to ride. I know this myself, because life was much more simple when I just had Zip. Now with Zip, Seattle and Trouble, I need help in the barn some days, and I really have to work at making riding and training a priority.

It's not only care that gets shortchanged. When you are short of time to ride, it's easy to miscalculate the amount of control you have of your horse. When training is inconsistent, we forget what we've done; we may assume that we've practiced a certain exercise enough, and we often end up frustrated or asking too much of our horses.

Because I'm on the road so much, I don't have much time for training. I keep Zip fit, I work with Seattle, and I play with Trouble when I get the chance. Recently I had "the boys" at Equitana and took advantage of a few minutes to work with Trouble around parking lot traffic. I don't want to find myself out on a ride assuming that because I can ride Trouble in the arena or on the trail, he's OK to take on the road. It's not fair to him, and it's dangerous. So sometimes training involves making the most of opportunities. We can do this by keeping our training program clearly in mind.

Whether you are training or caring for your horses, please remember they need time and care. Adjust your schedule or get help, but allow enough time to do a good job with your perfect horses. ▪PH▪

10

Just Say "Yes!"

When we have training problems, we analyze the problem, evaluate the goal, then develop a lesson plan, breaking the teaching process down into many baby steps. Each of these steps presents a series of questions, like a quiz at school. Because the teacher wants his student to succeed, he asks a lot of questions that the student can answer correctly. He is not trying to catch him making errors.

We can apply this to horse training. We're going to ask questions of the horse that he can answer with a "yes." If we get a "no," either we have asked a question that's too hard for him right now, or we have skipped a step in his training.

There are two ways we know we are getting a "yes." The first is that the horse does what we are asking. The second is that at the end of the lesson the horse is calmer than at the beginning. If we loaded a horse in a trailer, for instance, but he stands there a nervous wreck, we didn't get a "yes" answer. If we finally got a bit in the horse's mouth but it was a fight to do so, we didn't get a "yes" answer, either.

As you teach your horse to "give to the bit," for instance, you're teaching him to say "yes" to your rein. If you work along, doing the number of repetitions I recommend, you'll find that your horse will not only perform much better to your rein requests, but his overall performance will improve as he's conditioned to answer "yes." Interestingly enough, when we work on the giving exercises in the riders' clinics, we find the horses all learn to ground tie without our specifically teaching them to do it. Working on one thing helps another.

I think that our own Creator just wants us to say "yes" to Him, to acknowledge Him as God. Then other things change almost automatically. We don't tell our horse, "You go get yourself squared away and doing lots of trained-horse things, then come talk to me about being my horse." God doesn't ask us to clean up our act and do lots of religious things, either.

Just as we ask our horse for lots of little yesses, God only asks for little yesses from us. The result of our saying "yes" is that we are calmer and more peaceful, just as the horse is more peaceful when he learns to say "yes" to us consistently.

Think about just asking your horse to say "yes," and before long you'll find yourself riding down the trail with a perfect horse. ▣

11

Training Isn't Hard

If you head out to the barn, thinking to yourself, "Oh, gosh, this next lesson is gonna be tough," you'll end up making it hard for yourself and your horse. Horse training really isn't difficult. "I'll never be able to train" or "My horse must be the most stupid horse alive" can readily become "This is easy." How? By realizing that a goal is not the starting point in the training, and that we only need to get the horse to take one step at a time in the desired direction. By reducing a lesson into many mini-lessons, we can make

progress quickly and smoothly and, at the same time, avoid a wreck.

Let's say, for instance, that we have been working in the round pen and, despite our "shooing" our horse, we can't get him to move away from us. Is this a frustrating situation? Yes. But, is training this horse hard? No.

Instead of thinking about getting the horse to move away, think about making your request more specific — ask a front foot to take one step toward the fence. To ask for the movement, you might use a kiss or wave of the lariat. If that doesn't work, you could put the horse on a halter and lead rope and work on the WESN (directional control) lesson.

Training is difficult and complicated only when we aren't clear about what we want the horse to do. But by figuring out how to get one step in the direction we want, training becomes logical and easier.

To find simple solutions, we must break out of our mental corrals. In our round-pen example, most people would have presumed that putting the horse on a halter and lead was out of bounds. However, since we are not limited to one "right" method, we should actively search for ways to more specifically communicate to our horse what we want of him. We can apply this line of thinking to nearly any training dilemma.

For instance, do you have trailer-loading problems? Teach your horse the "go forward" cue, but teach him to step one foot forward on cue at the wash rack, where you can both be calm. If you are scared to ride your horse because he rears, teach him to drop his head on cue, but stay on the ground when teaching the lesson. Nothing says you have to be in the saddle to train.

And, like horse training, getting right with God isn't as hard as many people think. God asks a specific — one step in His direction with our heart. He hears and rewards a simple prayer, like we recognize the movement of our horse's front foot. Fortunately we have a model of adaptability to make it easy — our perfect horse. **PH**

12

The Whole Enchilada

"We want it all and we want it now!" That's human nature talking. If we are going to be good teachers to our horses, however, we'll have to adjust our thinking. We can have it all — just on a realistic timetable.

When I'm working with a horse, I look for ways to encourage him, to tell him, "You're on the right track." Sometimes that means that I have to accept part of what he did and work for the rest the next time.

If I get critical, he'll get discouraged or frightened, and I'll set him back. I want to build his confidence, then he'll be eager to work with me. With my thoroughness and his eagerness, we

can reach our goal. But, if the teacher loses the student's cooperation, it doesn't matter how well he or she knows the subject matter — they've lost the student.

Having said that, we don't reduce our expectations; we just
make sure we have a good lesson plan and enough repetitions that
the horse can eventually meet our expectations.

In each topic we study, we are going to ask ourselves what we
want the horse to do — what part of the horse we are trying to
control. Then we'll develop the step-by-step lesson plan we need
to achieve it. We'll have to ask ourselves if what we want from the
horse is a goal or a starting place. If it's not a starting place, then
we'll backtrack in our thinking to find a simple way to explain to
the horse what we want him to do. We can't demand the whole
enchilada at once.

Many of the letters I receive have to do with getting a horse to
slow down or stop, and almost everyone expects that to be an easy
thing to ask the horse to do. In reality, it's a result — not a starting point. Getting a horse to move his hip over may be a first step.

Sometimes good training involves looking at goals or problems
from different perspectives. For instance, consider the problem of
the horse who goes too fast. Instead of just putting on the brakes,
we can learn to adjust his speed — to gain control of the gas pedal.

It's always good to ask not just "How do we solve this problem?"
but "What performance are we looking for?" I work for improvement, not perfection, in each lesson.

Consistent improvement eventually leads to the whole enchilada
— the perfect horse! PH

13

When In Doubt — Quit

You probably know more about training and conditioning your horse than you think you do. If you listen to the little voice inside you, not relying exclusively on the advice of others when working a horse, you probably know what's safe and when it's time to quit.

It doesn't matter if we're talking about overtraining or riding down a muddy embankment. When the thought crosses your mind that your horse may be working too hard, stop working him. If you think he's struggling a little too much, then quit too — regardless of what advice you may be getting from a trainer or knowledgeable friend. You can't get hurt by quitting five minutes too soon, so stop. You can always resume training tomorrow. But you may well get hurt or get your horse hurt by quitting five minutes too late.

There are lots of factors to take into account, and none of them should be thought of as silly. The obvious ones include the weather and the footing, but more subtle ones have to do with your "hunch" that it's time to stop. Some people will tell you that you should push on through problems, and that you cannot stop until you are on a "positive note." That's nonsense.

You can stop whenever you think you should stop. I make it a point to always be within 20 seconds of quitting. If you stop working before you've gotten the horse to do a particular thing, he hasn't "gotten away" with anything. Since it takes a number of repetitions for a horse to learn a lesson, doing it once "right" isn't the most important thing. And it certianly isn't the most important thing if it means you've injured your horse getting him in the trailer or if you've gotten him across the creek, but then he injured someone when he took off.

Sometimes quitting is hard to do, even if we know it's the right thing. Our pride or fear of failure gets into the act. But sometimes knowing it's OK to quit gives you permission to begin. So work hard, but know when to quit working your perfect horse. ■PH■

14

Your Horse Will Let You Ruin His Performance

Did you know that you can take your horse from good performance to poor performance? It isn't hard to do. It's called discouragement, and you've probably experienced it yourself.

Imagine that you are working hard to please your boss. Instead of appreciating your effort, he keeps pushing for more performance. What happens? You stop trying so hard, and your performance slides. You may even end up doing a worse job than before he began "encouraging" you.

That happens with our horses, too. For instance, let's say that we are working on collection or lateral work. We ask the horse to go forward. When he does, we focus on getting sideways steps. As we focus more on the sideways steps, we end up slowing the horse — telling him to go, but not to go. His energy level goes down, his steps get smaller, and it gets harder to go sideways. So we get more intense with our requests.

What has happened? Two things. First, the horse didn't get frequent enough rewards for what he did right, so he assumed that he wasn't doing the right thing and got discouraged. Second, as he used muscles he may not ordinarily use, he began to hurt.

Does that mean that we shouldn't ask our horse to do anything hard? Of course not, but it does mean making sure we don't discourage him, and that we gradually condition him to do what we want, not expect a big performance all at once.

So when you are doing a maneuver that requires the horse to work in a way unfamiliar to him, imagine yourself going to the gym for the first time. Treat his muscles with respect. That's why, when we do the "giving to the bit" exercises, we let the horse relax and return his neck to a natural position occasionally. We don't ask him to hold a collected position until after he has developed the muscles to do so comfortably.

And when your horse makes a mistake, don't scold him. At least he's trying. You have to know the difference between how repetition develops a conditioned response and how overtraining kills a performance. Frequent releases and breaks make the difference.

We could take a lesson from a page in God's book for this. God isn't a taskmaster, asking us to do more with fewer rewards. It's just the opposite. He asks us for a relationship and provides us with the encouragement and support that a caring relationship provides. Be sure you are cheering your partner on, rather than discouraging him. After all, you can ruin the performance of even a perfect horse. ▣

15

Make The Good
Outweigh The Bad

Many of the training principles I use are straight from the Bible. Training is really about building good working relationships, and the Bible is the best relationship manual ever written, with clear-cut examples of what really works and what doesn't.

One major Biblical theme emphasizes overcoming evil with good, sometimes expressed even today as "loving your enemies" or doing good to those who hate you. On one level, especially in today's aggressive, hyper-competitive world, that advice may seem illogical. It makes sense, however, when you consider the effectiveness of turning on a light, rather than cursing the darkness — replacing what you don't want with something that you do. So, how does this concept apply to horse training?

Well, to change our horse's behavior when he does something we don't want, we must replace that activity with performance that we do want. It also tells us that scolding or punishing our horses for doing something "bad" won't work. We need to find ways to communicate (build a relationship) that make sense to the horse — ways in which he feels rewarded for cooperating with us, and ways that encourage him to change his own behavior (where we're not just restraining him from bad behavior).

For instance, have you ever noticed that horses who wear tie-downs always need those restraints? A tie-down doesn't change a horse's behavior — it only holds a bad habit at bay. But we can replace a horse's high-headed behavior by using "giving to the bit" exercises to teach him to carry his head calmly at the elevation we want.

Sometimes — for instance, when we work with a buddy-sour horse — we replace a horse's anxiousness with confidence and his panicky behavior with responses to our cues. Horses weren't made to "go it alone." Their deeply ingrained instincts tell them that they should stay with the band and trust the leader to keep them safe.

So, does that mean that we should let the horse do what he wants? Of course not. To build a relationship that is meaningful to our horse (and performance that will keep us safe, too), we have to convince him that he's safe with us. We can "show him who's boss," but in a positive way. We must build his confidence in our leadership and, especially, in our ability to care for him, to communicate with him, to keep him safe.

God doesn't want us — or our horses — to go through life afraid. In fact, He reassures us that His perfect love (which looks out for our best interests) displaces (replaces) fear. So as you make your lesson plans, in whatever terms you want to think of it, the good should outweigh the bad, and thoughtfulness and consideration should replace fear. It's the way we were designed to deal best with our perfect horses. ▣

16

Our Actions Tell The Truth

You've heard it said, "Actions speak louder than words." Well, it's true. Unfortunately, now more than ever, it seems people say one thing and do another — but it's not OK.

People walk up to me with their horse on a lead line, telling me what a great horse he is and how much they love him. Then without thinking, they jerk the lead for all they are worth when the horse does the slightest thing wrong.

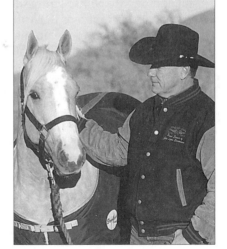

Others talk about respect for animals, but they speak disrespectfully of other's horses, calling them all kinds of offensive names. It's a way of life at some barns, cutting horses (and riders) down, as if pointing out flaws makes the person talking seem knowledgeable or important.

One of my pet peeves is people who hit their horses to praise them instead of stroking them. Horses don't appreciate being hit any more than people do. In fact, a horse's skin is much more sensitive than a person's. So, when you give him big slaps on the neck after a performance, it's no reward for the horse — in fact it's downright annoying — and it tells me that you care more about following the crowd than finding out what is important to your horse. If when you congratulate or praise your horse, you hear your hand make contact with him, you've hit him, not petted him.

I'm concerned about these types of inconsistencies as I hear stories of some horse trainers who claim to have special understanding of horse behavior, yet whose actions don't show the ordinary kindnesses. Interestingly enough, horse people don't seem to notice, but non-horsemen often do. They rightly ask, "If that guy loves that horse, why does he do what he's doing?" The horseman often explains away rude behavior in the name of some training technique.

And what about the more subtle forms of lack of respect, such as setting unrealistic performance goals? Or arbitrarily yelling "Quit!" and thumping on a horse when he does something you didn't like, instead of telling him what you want him to do. Would you like to live in a world where you learned what was OK to do by getting yelled at for everything you did wrong?

I'm glad our Heavenly Father doesn't treat us that way. He loves us and consistently shows it. He doesn't scold us when we do wrong — scolding never builds relationships — He forgives us and shows us a better way. In fact, one reason Jesus came to earth was to be an example. His actions and His words were consistent.

It doesn't matter if you're watching horse trainers or people in their ordinary lives — listen to what their actions say. Then be sure that your own actions and words are appropriate. Is anything less the right way to treat a perfect horse? **PH**

17

Zip In The Hall Of Fame

It's no secret that I'm proud of Zip. But a whole bunch of other people showed how proud they were of him too, on February 28, 1998, as Bright Zip was inducted into the Appaloosa Hall of Fame. I can't think of a more deserving horse, considering how consistent a performer and friend he's been through our many jobs together.

He started in the show ring as a yearling. Then for years he worked with me on the ranch, doctoring cattle, hauling irrigation pipes and everything that goes along with long days on a working cattle ranch. On weekends, we'd go to horse shows for fun. The last year we showed, he did so well that he was high-point performance horse in two clubs. We competed in 11 shows, and he was high point in 10. He's pretty versatile — Western pleasure, English classes, jumping, cattle classes and games.

But the hard work came when we began clinics. I snubbed him up to thousands of really difficult horses — stallions who wanted to fight, mares who wanted to kick his head off, and geldings who were pretty angry about life. Those horses were none too happy about me either, but Zip kept me safe. Whenever I needed to get out of a bind, or demonstrate a lesson, Zip was there.

And conditions weren't always easy for him. He's been trailered over a million miles. When we first went on the road, the trailers weren't as comfortable and quiet as they are now. And when we arrived somewhere, accommodations weren't plush. I remember on one trip into Canada, he had to stay in a pig pen with the pigs. Through all of that he has never been sick, his legs have stayed good, and his attitude has never changed.

Even when he went blind from an anaphylactic reaction, nothing really changed. He was brave enough to carry on as usual, though he couldn't see. Now he still runs at full speed, spins and works bridleless. Though I'm careful not to put him in situations where his lack of vision could get him hurt, I still snub horses up to him. Those horses don't know that he can't see; they are just as aggressive as ever, and Zip maintains his balance and keeps us both safe.

Being in the Hall of Fame is really a special honor for him, though it certainly won't go to his head. In fact, one of the things so special about Zip is that nothing goes to his head — he's the same horse every time I work with him. I can't begin to tell you the encouragement I've received from him and how God has used Zip to teach me life lessons. Zip's pretty special, and it's good to honor our good performers, but even without any training he'd be just like the horse in your backyard — a perfect horse. PH

18

Zip's Not My Horse

Bright Zip isn't my horse. He's God's horse, just on loan to me. Likewise, the horse in your barn isn't really yours. God just gave him to you to care for and love. And because our horses belong to God, you and I will have to give an account someday for how we've treated them. But that isn't bad.

If you had something really valuable — a fragile family treasure, for instance — would you give it to your child when he was three years old? Of course not. Would you give it to him at 16, when he has trouble just keeping his room straight, or at 22 when he finishes college and you know he'll most likely be moving around the country, packing and unpacking? Probably not. If it was something you really treasured, you'd wait until your child was settled and able to appreciate it. By the time you give it to him, you'd be sure that he could care for it.

The horse is to God like that family treasure is to you. Horses are important to God, so He put within each of us the knowledge of what is right and wrong to do with them, so that we could care for them well. We may not instinctively know how much to feed or how often they need shoes — we have to learn the specifics. But we do know, for instance, when a trainer tells us he wants to tie the horse's head around to the stirrup for 10 hours, that isn't right. Or when someone wants to hit a horse with a 2 x 4 to "teach" him a lesson, something in your gut says that isn't acceptable. We have to learn to trust our instincts when it comes to how to treat our horses right.

But does that mean we'll never make mistakes? No. God knew that, too, so when he made the horse, He not only included traits like beauty and courage; He also included adaptability and forgiveness. If that's how much God cares for His horses, imagine how much more He cares for us.

Back to the family heirloom, if you just wanted it to be safe, you'd put it in a vault. But because you wanted to share something of yourself, you gave it to your child. That's some of why God gave us horses. He wanted us to see how their beauty, courage and, especially, forgiveness is a reflection of Himself. So next time you have a decision to make regarding your horse, remember that God loved you enough to give you the horse, and He loves the horse enough to give you insight into how to treat him. And God planned that we fully enjoy our perfect horses. ▄PH▄

19

Boring Becomes Exciting

Boring — that's how some people describe good horse training. Asking a horse to do something hundreds of times can be boring. But then there are the alternatives — wrecks aren't boring. Runaways don't put you to sleep, and you are more likely to get angry than bored trying to force-load a horse into a trailer.

People come to my clinics and can't believe that they'll spend three full days learning the same exercise, and sometimes only at the walk. By the end of the clinic, they are amazed how much they've learned, but they are also tired. Concentrating for that long a time and fighting boredom can be tough. But dealing with their horse's bad behavior hundreds of times without resolving anything can get old, too.

The first time you try a new exercise, you'll be concentrating on remembering the procedure and watching the horse to see his reactions, to see if he's understanding your message. When he does what you ask, it's thrilling. It's tempting to quit then and go enjoy an iced tea — or to move ahead to lesson two. But really, the work on lesson one is just beginning.

Horses have learning cycles. They are *bad*, then *good*, then *real bad* for a long time, then much *better*, then *bad* for a short time, and finally, *good consistently*. The final stage is when you know the horse has learned the lesson.

The first *good* feels great — but the horse has just happened to try an option that was the right one. He doesn't know the lesson, and he may not know that he gave the correct answer. The *bad* phase is just around the corner. Expect it, and don't blow your cool when it comes. You have to train your horse through the *bad* phase with the same carefulness and concentration that you did through the first *good* phase. And then stick with him.

It's not miraculous

Have you ever gone to a clinic with a miracle-worker trainer? Your horse does super. You always knew he was a good horse, and today you are proud to own him. You bring him home. The next day you can't get to square one, and you feel like a failure. You're not a failure, and the trainer probably wasn't a miracle worker. He probably just stopped at the *good* phase.

Clinicians are under pressure to get results. Owners are impatient and want to see something happen. I've been in that situation before. In a demonstration, I've had to start a colt and ride him within a few minutes. I do it, but I don't pretend the horse is trained or that the owner can go on from there. I always tell that owner that they need to go back and really teach the horse.

People go through learning cycles, too. Imagine a teenager with a curfew of 9 p.m. First few nights, all's fine — in by 9. Next night or two it's 9:30 and 9:20 (of course, with the usual excuses). Family discussion follows. Next few nights nine-ish, with one 8:50 just to keep the average low. Suddenly it's 10:30 or 11 before the teenager appears. Big blow up. Every night thereafter is 9 p.m. or else the teenager stays home all evening. Lesson learned.

When your horse is acting up or when you are getting frustrated, think about the teenager analogy. Are you or your horse just having a 10:30 day? We sometimes say, "But he knew it yesterday. Why is he being a jerk today?" He didn't know it yesterday. He just got lucky a few times, and if he knew the right answer, he'd give it to you.

Could it be that when you got a little bored, you got sloppy, in effect changing your signals and complicating things for him? Maybe there's a fine line between bored and frustrated. It doesn't take talent to be a great trainer. It takes consistency and willingness to work through an exercise hundreds of times.

I've been told that the Chinese did a study in preparation for the Olympics. They determined that it takes between 100,000 and 200,000 times for a movement to become a subconscious response. We are trying to develop a conditioned or subconscious response in our horses. If we pick up on the rein, we don't want them to have to guess what that means. We want to bypass the questioning mechanism and go straight to the mechanism of the conditioned response. So that takes teaching the lesson and repeating the request, response and release hundreds, maybe thousands, of times until the horse has it down pat.

Even then, if you expect your horse to go 15 minutes without getting heavy on the rein, you'll be disappointed. With wrong expectations, you'll likely react adversely, damaging the relationship you have with your horse. Instead, realize that just as we're "only human," your horse is "only a horse," and he's going to be inconsistent. That's why we have to keep working with him, training him and reminding him of what we want him to do, but not scolding him for his mistakes.

God works with us the same way. He knows we are not perfect, so He guides us onto the best path, taking care to remind us of His love along the way. Reviewing the basics can be boring, but it can also become pretty exciting as we find a great relationship developing with our perfect horse. ■

Notes

Section II

Dear John ...

20

Dear John: Answers To Your Ground Handling Questions

Everyone runs into questions during the course of training their horse. Many of those fall into the form of "Am I doing the right thing?" or "What do I do next?" The best thing to do in those cases is always fall back on the training principle: Determine what you can do with the horse and be 100-percent safe and have him respond correctly 100 percent of the time. That will give you a safe, solid starting point for your lesson, and the next step will be easier to see.

Now a convert

My first reaction to your magazine was "Yeah, right." I'd heard of John Lyons but didn't know anything about your methods. I've worked with horses for 21 years and have never had a horse I could not train. After reading Perfect Horse *for over a year, I see how untrained and out of control my horses actually were (and how fortunate I was to not have wrecked).*

Now a stay-at-home mom with three pre-school children, I don't have time to ride, so I decided to start the round-pen training on my 10-year-old broodmare and her two-year-old son, a gelding. What I find amazing is that after three weeks of just the basic "getting the feet to move" and direction changes, their personalities seem to have changed. They now stand back a respectful distance during grain time. And the mare — who has always been one to drag me to every blade of grass — is much less pushy.

I don't have a round pen, just a rectangular corral, so I have to move with the horses to keep them moving. If I accidentally over-shoot the hip and move toward the shoulder area or take my eye off the hip and even look toward their head or nose, they try to turn. I didn't ask for the turn, but I may have inadvertently cued them with my body and eyes. Who is in control?

JH/Owensville, MO

We're glad that the round-pen training is producing good results for you. Most people report that their horses are more "respectful" after working them in the round pen. This is because respect is a byprod-uct of control — when the horse learns that you can control him without causing him pain, he begins to respect your leadership and to trust you. So your horse's performance tells you that you are on a right track.

The real advantage to a round pen is that there are no corners for a horse to get "stuck" in, so the horse always has someplace to go. You can use the round-pen techniques with a small pen of any shape, or even on the lead rope, so the shape of the pen is probably not a

I use the minimum stimulation necessary to get the horse to move, beginning with simple body language and the rope. If the horse doesn't move, then I become more energetic. If I "chase" the horse to get him to go, I'll have to "chase" him every time. My objective is to get him to do more on lighter cues.

problem. If the pen is too large, it may be difficult to stay close enough to your horse. (The ideal diameter for a round pen is 60 feet.)

You might try getting the horse to move without physically chasing him every step — and that may help the problem of overshooting your cue spot. I use the minimum stimulation necessary to get the horse to do what I want, because I want the horse to respond to increasingly subtle cues.

If your horse isn't doing what you want him to do, you're not in control. It's normal for the horse to attempt to change directions. In fact, only until he tries to change and you make him change back so he goes the direction you want does he realize that you are in control. Up until then, he thinks that he's moving on his own.

Since a cue is a signal that you specifically teach the horse. You are not mis-cueing your horse; he just has not learned to go consistently in the direction you ask. You've done the first and second part of the training principles — getting the horse's feet to move, and to move consistently. Now you have to work on the next part — getting the horse's feet to move in the direction that you want.

Round pen for mules too?

I just bought my first mule to trail ride and pull a wagon. By using your round-pen method, will I be able to reach my goal? Do you do anything different when training a mule than a horse?
Christie/Internet

Yes, I would use the round pen, but I'm always more careful with a mule not to put the mule in a situation where he learns a behavior I don't want, like dragging me off at the end of a lead rope. If he's allowed to do this three or four times, it may take me two weeks to a month of consistent work to get that thought out of his mind. Mules remember escape routes better and longer than horses.

Mules are extremely intelligent animals. John has worked with a number of mules over the years, and he says they have a great memory for escape routes.

Distracted stallion

Can you tell me how you keep Zip quiet when he's around a mare? My stallion is a joy to ride — unless there's a mare within five miles of him. Then he drives me crazy hollering to her. I've tried hitting him or spurring him when he does that, but it doesn't do any good.
KM/Scottsdale, AZ

Use the same philosophy you would to keep your teenage kids from being overly preoccupied with the other sex — keep them working or engaged in a hobby. That's why so many parents have gotten their kids involved with horses, because it gives them a healthy outlet for their energy and can help keep them out of trouble.

Get your horse really involved in what you want him to be doing, and the other unwanted behavior will disappear after a while.

Years ago, I scolded Zip when he hollered at a mare, but I've figured out much better ways since then. He can't break at the poll, move his shoulder over, move on the diagonal at the lope and still be hollering. If he is doing what I want and he still has enough attention on other matters to be yelling, then I increase the demand, for instance, making more and quicker transitions.

But if I spend my time chewing on another person — whether it is my horse or kids — it doesn't build our relationship or help them do the right thing. An occasional word of correction or reminder is one thing. I'll sometimes tell Zip, "Hey!" But I don't punish him for what is natural, and I never jerk on the reins to tell him not to talk to other horses.

Won't stand for shots

We own two horses. One stands for shots well, the other does not. Is there anything we can do to help him get through his upcoming visit by the vet and vaccinations?

Last week the horse who doesn't take shots well got vasculitis, and the vet gave him a shot to bring the swelling down. When she stuck the needle in his neck, his head went way up in the air, his front feet came off the ground, and you could see the fear in his eyes. (We had tied him to the stall bars so he wasn't loose.) It took a while to calm him down enough to be able to give him the medication. Even though we talked to him calmly, he still was scared.

VP/Internet

As frustrating as this problem is, it's not insurmountable, and you are doing the right thing in working with the horse before the vet gets there. For the sake of discussion, forget about how the horse acts now, but think about how you want him to act. No doubt you want him to stand still, without dancing around. You'd like him to keep his head at a relaxed height, and to drop it on cue if he raises it too high. You want him to step forward on cue when he wants to step back. And you want the vet to be able to approach him without him panicking.

Move and countermove
We can't make a horse stand still. We can teach him to move any of four directions on cue, so that when he makes a move on his own, we can ask him to make the countermove. So if he backs, we can tell him to go forward. We do that without pulling on the halter, because it's his feet that we're talking to, not his head.

When he moves forward, as if he would rush past us, we can tell him to back up. If he moves left, we can ask him to move right, and vice versa. (Each of those movements are separate lessons, but used together we can refer to it as the WESN lesson.) So we're going to handle the standing-still problem by asking the horse to move counter to how he moves on his own.

When a horse learns to step each of four directions on cue, we can ask him for a countermove when he makes a move we don't want.

After a while, when we give him the opportunity to stand still, he'll take advantage of it.

When you have a situation like this, you can start out with one problem — shots — and end up with two problems — shots and the horse pulling back when tied, even when he's not getting shots. So begin in a calm environment with the horse not tied.

When the horse is upset, scared or excited, his head will automatically go up. When he drops his head, he'll automatically relax. Another benefit of dropping his head, of course, is that his front feet stay on the ground, so you can solve the rearing problem and high-head or stiff-neck problem at the same time.

We're going to use pressure on the top of the horse's head as a cue to tell him to drop his head. You can do this one of two ways. The first is to rest your hand on the top of the horse's head. When the horse moves his head up, keep your resting pressure the same. The moment the horse moves his head down — even a quarter of an inch — leave your hand where it is so the horse can drop his head away from it, or else raise your hand. Either way, you are releasing the horse from the pressure (although it's light) of your hand on his head. That will tell him that he did the right thing. Pet the horse and begin again. Walk away, then back to the horse and begin again.

When a horse wants to avoid being clipped, vaccinated, de-wormed or even bridled, it's best to look at the problem in light of "what cue do I wish he was obeying?" rather than "he's afraid of the clippers."

It's likely that if you are having this problem, the horse may also be headshy, so it may not be so easy to rest your hand on his head. The other way to reach the same objective is by attaching a lead rope to the bottom ring of the halter and pulling slightly downward on his halter. That will put pressure on the top of his head. Keep your pressure light, but steady, even when he raises his head (don't increase the pressure when he raises it, just go with him, keeping pressure on the lead rope). The moment he drops his head, release the pressure. This will take lots of repetition, but eventually the horse will automatically drop his head when he feels pressure on it. So then you'll have taught him to stand and to drop his head.

One other thing you may want to consider is the sacking-out lessons. Again, don't have the horse tied, but put him on a lead line so that you have some control. Or you can do this in a round pen. Approach him with something not-too-scary, like a washcloth. Pet him one or two strokes on the shoulder, then walk away with it, before the horse pulls away. You want to begin with something so low threat that the horse will do what you want him to do — stand there relaxed — then withdraw the "threat" before he does what you don't want him to do. Walk up to the horse again, pet him one or two strokes with the cloth, then walk away. Repeat this lots of times until he stays really relaxed with it.

Then you can begin walking up to him with more scary things, petting him, then walking away. The walking away is important because it tells the horse that he's off duty, that he can relax again. By doing so, you are conditioning him to relax after he's gotten worried. You are also letting him know that the threat only lasts for seconds. He learns he can live through it for three or four or five seconds, so he learns to delay getting upset. No sense getting upset to have to relax again, to get upset again and so forth. So the horse's emotional control is being conditioned.

Walking away from the horse is also really important because it gives you the opportunity to walk back up to him — since that's what the vet will eventually have to do.

Emotional control
Once the horse has learned to stand, drop his head on cue and be approached with a scary thing without moving away while he's in a relaxed setting, then you'll have to make it more exciting. You want to condition his response even when he's scared or worried. Start out easy, just increasing the intensity of one thing at a time. It may be that you have been working with him outside where he feels relaxed. You might bring him into the barn aisle (where bad stuff

has happened previously) and begin with the WESN lesson, so that he doesn't feel trapped. When he can stand easily, ask him to drop his head. When that goes well, step away from him, then approach again with the same washcloth in your hand. Build the lesson like that — adding only one exciting element at a time.

LYONISM ...

HORSES SEEK OUR LEVEL. IF I AM SATISFIED WITH MY HORSE WALKING TO ME WHEN I CALL HIM, THEN HE WILL NEVER RUN TO ME. MY HORSE IS SATISFIED WHEN I AM SATISFIED.

Once your horse will stand with his head relaxed and drop his head on cue even if you rush up to him with a crinkly paper bag, then get someone else into the act. Have them walk up to the horse with just the washcloth as you previously. Build his confidence and response to cues so well that he can stand without getting upset even when a stranger approaches with a strange object.

When the vet comes, ask her to approach, pet him and step away several times (only takes about 30 seconds). Then ask her to approach and pet him but not move away too quickly (another 30-40 seconds). When the horse has had a chance to settle and realize that she's not going to trap him and attack him, he should be considerably better about getting a shot, which only lasts a few moments.

This takes lots of repetition, but it's worth it in the end. It's natural for us to focus on the injection as being the problem, but in the horse's mind, it's probably the entire experience — getting tied, scared, etc. — and then the injection is worse than if he took the experience in stride. Make sure you don't scold him for his frightened behavior, but just concentrate on asking him to do what you want of him. So, "Quit!" won't tell him what you want him to do, but "Step left" will.

If you don't take the time to deal with this behavior, you'll find it showing up in situations other than just shots, and you'll end up blaming the horse for being "difficult" or "stubborn," when in reality it's fear and lack of training. When horses are scared, we owe it to them to help them over their fear.

Unbridling problems

My mare gets scared when we take the bridle off. In the past, when the crownpiece was removed from behind her ears, she would immediately throw her head up. The bit would then fall forward and get hung up on her bottom teeth. Sometimes she would hold the bit in her mouth before releasing it and then throw her head.

Now, when I unbridle her, I can get her to lower her head, but even with her head down, she becomes tense and throws her head when the bit is released.

We have had her teeth checked and have eliminated dental problems as a source of her difficulty. What can I do to keep her from throwing her head?

TM/Bakersfield, CA

Horses who get scared as you unbridle them have usually had their teeth hit with the bit. You are on the right track by teaching your mare to drop her head on cue. When her head comes up, ask her to drop it again, and again. Then work with her mouth and norse until you can put your fingers in and out of her mouth easily.

Then put a cotton rope in place of the bit and work on taking that out. That way, if she jumps or throws her head, the "bit" isn't going to hurt her teeth and scare her. When she's pretty relaxed with that, work with a real snaffle bit, taping a washcloth around it so if it happens to hit her teeth, it won't hurt.

When taking the bridle off, be sure to maintain control so the bit does not hit the horse's teeth.

It will take time, but when she is confident that you won't hurry her as you pull the bridle away and is reassured that the bit won't hurt her, she'll learn to relax and hold her head down.

Itchy head problem

About six months ago I purchased a seven-year-old Paint. He rides, clips, bathes and loads very well. But I have one problem that I don't know how to solve: He has a habit of taking his head and rubbing it on anyone nearby, as if to scratch himself. When he has a bit in his mouth, this can be dangerous for me! Any suggestions you could give me would be greatly appreciated.

RD/Internet

This is a problem similar to a puppy jumping up on his owner — sometimes it doesn't bother the owner, but other times it's irritating or potentially dangerous. The problem with the horse, like with a puppy, is that the owner will have to become consistent in what behavior is OK, if the animal is to make changes. If, for instance, you allow the horse to rub his head on you following a long ride on a hot day after the bridle is taken off, then he's not going to understand that he can't do the same thing whenever he wants. So the first step in changing the horse's behavior is determining what behavior is acceptable, and then expecting it consistently.

Second, swatting at the horse doesn't help. In fact, anytime we scold or "discipline" our horse, we end up with behavior that we don't want, such as our horse throwing his head. We can't control our horse's behavior with "don't" cues. By the time we can tell the horse "Don't," it's too late.

I suggest one or both of two options: The first is to give the horse more attention than he wants. Each time he attempts to rub his head on you, hold his nose or head and rub it between your two hands — not hard, just enough to bug him. If you do that regularly, he'll think, "Gee, every time I try to rub my head, my nose gets rubbed more than I enjoy. I think I'll keep my nose where those folks can't bother it."

The other option is to think about a behavior you want from your horse — like improved halter manners — and work on that behavior each time he nudges you with his head. When he comes nosing around, ask him to step his hip over or to back two steps. Then he'll get the idea he has to work when he invades your space in a pushy way, and he'll prefer to stand near you quietly.

Another thing that will help is to not stand too close to him or to fuss with his nose/head too often when you are just standing idle. For the mouthy or pushy horse, it's like putting a kid's hand in the cookie jar and telling him not to touch a cookie. Sometimes owners inadvertently encourage that pushy behavior. Nothing's wrong with smooching after the horse learns boundaries for smooching back and he learns not to be pushy.

Kicking foal

We have a 10-day-old filly who is very friendly. The problem is she quickly turns her backside to us and kicks out. I see her do this to her dam and guess she's only playing, but we want to stop this behavior before someone gets kicked.

MN/Palos Heights, IL

Kicking out and roughhousing are normal activities for babies to do, but you are right in not encouraging the behavior. Get in the habit of moving her away from you, not you backing away from her. As in basic round-pen work, the beginning of control is getting the feet to move — and at this point she probably has your feet moving.

The kicking behavior is easy to stop. When she turns as if she's going to kick, chase her a step or two away from you. You can throw something, like a water bucket or halter, at her to scare her. You don't want it to actually hit her, just make a noise landing behind her. It will only take a few times, and then she'll think before she fires with her back feet.

Crosstie trouble

I recently purchased a six-year-old Thoroughbred off the track. In the month that I've had him, we've worked on round-pen lessons, sacking out and the "go forward" and "yield to pressure" cues. He responds well on the halter, but the problem is that he pulls back when he's on the crossties.

When he begins to back up, I tap on his hip, giving him the "go forward" cue, and he'll step forward. But it occurred to me that if he feels the halter pressure on the top of his head, I should not have to ask him to step forward — he should do that on his own. Oddly enough, he doesn't pull back when being led, and his lungeing is going well. I only see the problem on the crossties. I've even tried only using one tie. That seems better, but not the solution, as he broke free with that, too.

When he breaks free, I put his breakaway halter back on him, tie him to one crosstie and resume grooming, without scolding him. What can I do to break this pattern?

KS/Internet

First, you are to be complimented on how well you've thought through the problem and the solutions you've tried so far. And you are 100 percent correct to not scold the horse. We never want to scold a horse who's tied or crosstied. That can create the very problem we're trying to cure.

Your approach of telling the horse to step forward (driving him forward from his hip with the "go forward" cue, rather than pulling on the cross ties) won't solve the problem with a confirmed puller, but it is a good way to show the horse what you want him to do. He learns that when he steps forward, the pressure releases.

Using one tie is a good idea as it's more forgiving than two ties, but as you know, it doesn't really solve the problem, either.

More groundwork

You are on the right track with all your ground-control exercises, including lungeing. Let's just review the "go forward" and the "give to pressure" cues before I give you an additional two exercises.

Stand as if you were about to lunge the horse to the left, but with your left hand only a few inches below the halter. With a stiff dressage whip, tap the top of the horse's left hip. Continue tapping lightly and rhythmically until the horse moves one of his feet forward. This gives you a way to drive him forward, rather than pulling him forward.

Once the horse is walking, put light pressure on the lead rope to ask him to stop. Keep the pressure steady until the horse slows his feet, then release the rope. The horse learns that when he does what you want of him, the pressure on the rope is released.

Once we've taught our horse to "yield to pressure" on the lead line when he's calm, we'll have to do that when he's excited, because he's going to get excited and scared when he pulls back and feels trapped by the pressure the halter puts on his head. You want him to learn that he can get scared, but he doesn't have to panic, and that he has a way to release the pressure himself.

Tell the horse to go forward as you did before, then let out the line and get way behind him so he's moving directly away from you. Pull on the rope as you did when he was beside you, so that he bends his neck and turns his nose toward you. Continue pulling until he turns entirely around to face you (not a circle, but a 180-degree turn, as in the photo on the next page). Walk up to him and pet him.

Send him away again, this time a little faster, and put a little more pressure on the line. You want to work up so you can have the horse canter away from you, then you put lots of pressure quickly on the rope and he'll bend his neck and turn around to face you. He's then yielding to pressure when he's excited.

Another approach
In addition to dealing with excitement, we want to put an additional step in the lesson plan so that we're sure the horse won't panic if he suddenly feels a big pressure. Our goal is to have the horse come forward when he feels pressure on the lead. But because our goal isn't our starting point, we can try the lesson from a different approach.

Normally we put tension on a line, be it the lead rope or the rein, hold that pressure steady until the horse does what we want, then we release the pressure. But this next exercise takes a different approach.

Put a lead rope on the horse and stand the lead's length away from the horse, facing him. Put about a half-ounce of pressure on the line, so there's no slack in it. Then suddenly pull hard on it and release

To cue the horse to go forward, we tap up high on his hip, then stop tapping as soon as he moves a foot forward. With repetition, the horse learns that your tap — and eventually, even your focus — on his hip is the signal to move forward.

Sometimes this lesson doesn't look very pretty because we work up to putting a lot of pressure on the horse suddenly. But he'll put himself under a lot of pressure if he gets startled and pulls back on the crossties. Eventually the horse will end up coming toward you instead of pulling back when you pull on the rope.

it immediately. When the horse feels the sudden pressure, he'll pull his head up, maybe even pull back, but he won't panic because the pressure will have already ended. After about 50 to 100 times, the horse will move toward you when you pull on the line.

It works like this: The first few times you pull, the horse will pull back. Because we released before he had a chance to resist, we essentially created a controlled-panic situation. As you continue the pull-and-release pattern, he'll pull less and less vigorously, until he'll just stand there as you tug on him then release the line. (The tugs we are talking about are as if you are trying to tow him, or to drag his nose toward you — hard pulls, but not jerks.)

A curious thing will happen a number of repetitions past when he doesn't pull back. He'll drop his head and begin to walk forward. You'll have replaced the horse's natural tendency to pull back when he feels pressure on the poll with a conditioned response to move his head forward. And the pattern of pulling back when tied — or crosstied — should be a thing of the past. Naturally, the horse may still get frightened and pull back on occasion until you really have this down pat.

Pulling back when tied isn't a habit people have to live with. Not tying the horse hard and fast won't keep them or the horse safe, either. When a horse has the level of fear that a horse who pulls back has, it's going to show up when you least want it to. The good news is that even confirmed pullers can be transformed into calm horses who are safe to tie.

Whip shy

One major obstacle I have with teaching the "go forward" cue is that my 16-year-old Appy mare is scared of a whip. I'm not sure why she is so scared, but I have seen her flee at a horse show when a whip was cracked while another horse was being lunged. Her previous owner made it a point to have me promise that I would not use a whip near her. Can you help here?

BL/Internet

None of the training I recommend is dependent on using a whip; the whip is just a tool. You can adapt the technique and use anything that gets the horse's feet moving, like a lariat.

But because the horse is afraid of whips and you can't always control the environment she'll find herself in, it's important to help her get over her fear. If a horse is afraid of something, and we know of it, we have an obligation to help them get over it, if we can. Otherwise, we risk them hurting themselves, us, and potentially other people or horses if they panic.

Start by holding something small, like a match stick while standing beside your horse. When she doesn't move, then walk away, with the match stick. Next, stand there with a pencil, or something about that size, then walk away. Build up from there, using your imagination as you increase the size of the object, until you can hold a whip and have her stand still comfortably.

The objective is for her to stand quietly. If you think she'll move her feet in four seconds, you should walk away with the object in three seconds — you want to set her up to do the right thing each time.

Then start moving the object, first the match stick, then the pencil, tarps, tin cans tied together and other similar objects. You'll want to move the object, make noise with it, stroke her with it, drop it on the ground, pass it to someone else, move it quickly, and so forth.

You do want to scare her, but only slightly — not so much that she moves. You are not getting her accustomed to things, but teaching her what to do when she's afraid. By following the pattern of exposing her to the scary item, then withdrawing it before she moves, the time she is able to stand without reacting will get longer and longer. Eventually you'll have a horse who doesn't spook — even at whips.

The more fear the horse has, the longer it may take, but teaching her how to deal with fear is one of the kindest things you can do.

Ballistic at horseflies

My three-year-old Quarter Horse filly is normally good minded. However, if a horsefly gets near her, she goes ballistic, kicking out with both hind feet. I board her at a stable where there is lots of activity, and I'm afraid someone may get hurt.

I can distract her when I'm riding, but not when I'm on the ground. When she starts kicking, I try to discipline her by snapping the lead rope, but she gets scared, runs backward and rears. I can't hold her. We don't have a round pen, so I work her in an arena.

I'm at a loss. She's thin-skinned, and when the horseflies bite her she gets huge welts, so I can't fault her for overreacting. Last year I rode her in the hottest part of the afternoon when fewer flies were out. Evenings are horrible because the flies are relentless.

KE/Fulton, MO

If you can control your filly when riding but not on the lead rope, that tells you she needs more work on the lead — more halter training and ground manners. You want her to be so well conditioned to your signals that she can obey you despite the distractions.

Also, don't snap the lead rope. When you do, the horse behaves in a way you don't want — as you found out. You snap the lead — she gets scared, pulls back, rears and runs away from you. So you have to change what you do, as well as train her. Teach her to "give to pressure" so that when she begins to pull back on the lead rope and feels pressure on the top of the halter, she'll move forward to release the pressure.

Also work with the spook-in-place lesson so she learns it's OK to get scared, but not to move her feet when she's scared.

Work on the WESN leading lesson so that you have good control of each movement. When she wants to move left, you can ask her to step right, and so forth.

Do lots of sacking out so that she gets comfortable with things around her body, legs and feet. You'll want to work up to throwing ropes and feed bags around her hindquarters and feet, not to hurt or to scare her but to teach her to stand when those things happen.

Just riding in the heat of the day won't solve the training problem, and before long she'll be pulling back about things other than flies if you don't teach her what behavior you expect.

Three at a time

I have to lead three horses at a time to their day pasture. Time does not permit me to lead one at a time. Each one leads great by themselves, but I have trouble with all three nipping at each other and dragging on me. I know it can be done. My grandfather would lead two teams of draft horses with no trouble. I have tried to go back to basics with all three individually but still have trouble with them together. Could you give me any suggestions?

PW/Internet

Time is a great pressure on each of us, but it's important that we don't let the factor of time push us into doing things that we know put us or our horses in danger. When we say we don't have enough time to do something right, we may be endangering ourselves or our horses. Not having enough time is like saying, "I know I'm out of control and might get hurt." We can't afford to take that risk. It's

It's a joy to be able to lead two well-behaved horses at the same time — but it doesn't happen without training.

John enjoys "playing" with the boys — Seattle and Trouble.

important to realize that when we think we're saving time, we often cost ourselves the most time. Sometimes this results in accidents. It's when we are hurrying that we do thing like run the tractor into the barn or tear up the equipment — and sometimes the "equipment" may be us.

It might take five minutes longer for you to walk each horse individually out to the pasture, but if one horse should pull away and you have to go catch him, or one horse kicks another and you have to wait for the vet, you'll have lost more than the initial 10 minutes. So, until you have the three horses under good control, I wouldn't advise leading them all at the same time.

To deal with the leading problem, pick the horse that leads the worst or acts up the most, and work with him individually. Raise your expectations of how he should lead and how responsive he should be to the halter and the lead rope. Then choose a day when you have an extra hour or two and take that horse along with the horse who leads the best, and work with the two of them. Get these two horses to where they are leading great together, so you have good control of them if one starts to chew on the other or if they start to act up, so you can correct the one who's causing the problem.

Then alternate with the best horse and the second-best horse, the worst horse and the second-best horse and so forth. When you are positive that you have good control on any two of the horses, put the three together.

Whenever they start to act up, focus all of your attention on the one who is acting up at that moment. Really get that one fixed, then do the next in line. So, if the horse on the far right starts acting up, put the other two horses in your other hand and focus on getting that horse paying attention to you. Do just what is necessary to hold onto the other two. Once you get that horse back under control and he's listening really well, then go to the next one. You can't do a little bit to each horse; you need to focus 100 percent of your attention on whatever horse is not behaving correctly.

You could also work the three horses in the round pen, starting with one, then adding another, then the other, as if you were training circus horses. It's pretty neat to watch, but it requires a lot of concentration on your part.

This same concept applies if you are trying to catch several horses in a field. If you have 10 horses in the field, you should only work with one, and let the other nine do whatever they want. Keep eye contact with the one you are working with. When you focus on that horse, controlling his direction even though he's influenced by his buddies, you'll eventually catch him. Then proceed through the herd, one at a time. Pretty soon you'll have caught all 10 horses, but if you just jump from one horse to the next, you'll be out there all day.

To intervene or not

Six months ago I bought a 10-year-old gelding who, among six or so horses, was lowest in the pecking order, as evidenced by many bite marks on his rump and flanks. Now, he's just with my husband's docile, easy-going gelding who loves everyone.

There is no longer a struggle for his own hay or grain, but he persists in bullying the 15-year-old by biting him and pushing him to move constantly. At the sound of grain, his ears pin back and at the sight of hay, his tail swishes.

Could I intervene and maybe end this behavior by refusing to feed him until his ears are forward? He's a wonderful horse otherwise.

JN/Spencer, MA

No, do not withhold the feed. One of the criteria for deciding if a training technique will work is whether we can provide correction/redirection when the need arises. Pasture problems are difficult because we can't provide 24-hour, seven-day-a-week training. Without that kind of consistency, whatever training we're using is bound to fail. So, if you are trying to have the horse act nicely toward the other horse overall, unless you spend 24 hours in the pasture everyday, you are not going to change his behavior.

What you can do is to train the horse to respond a certain way when *you* are in the pasture. If you can't control him when you are there, you are at risk both from your horse getting aggressive toward you and from getting run over by the other horse as he tries to get away from the aggressor. And, though he only picks on the other horse and hasn't hurt anyone yet, don't wait until he does.

Take the problem horse out of the pasture and work him, either in a round pen or on a halter and lead, getting better control and developing his ground manners. That involves leading manners, telling the horse to move his hips over, his shoulders over, and so forth. When you have good control with and without a halter on, then put him back in the pasture without the other horse, and continue the same exercises. Then ask him to obey you with the other horse present and eventually even without a halter. Don't let yourself get between the two horses until you're sure you can control the bossy one.

When you feed, give him his feed, but then stay by him while he's eating, rubbing on his head and neck (not his body). That shows the horse he can relax and eat while you're around. That way he'll become less grumpy about his feed.

If you feel like he's getting too aggressive when you feed, yell at him or throw the feed bucket at him, correcting him on the spot. Then, put his halter and lead on, lead him up to the feed and pet him as he eats.

First time wearing boots

I want to begin working with a horse in the round pen and put protective boots on him, as you recommend, but he's never had his feet worked with. How can I put the boots on without getting kicked or him getting upset?

PD/Humble, TX

I run into that problem often at my symposiums, when the "unbroke" horse I'm going to use for demonstration hasn't had his feet picked up or hasn't worn boots. I'll start rubbing the horse's neck, then step back to his nose. Then rub his shoulder, then back to his nose, then down toward his knee and back to his nose. I may brush along his shoulder with my shoulder, then go back to his nose. Pretty soon I can brush my hand down to his knee. Then I go back to his nose. Before long I'm brushing my hand down his leg longer and longer, each time going back to pet his nose.

I rub the leg pretty aggressively, then back to the nose. Then squeeze the leg a little and, of course, go back to the horse's nose.

I use the same pattern with his back legs, each time going back to his nose. I'll open and close the Velcro on the boot several times, so the horse gets used to the sound. By then, putting the boots on isn't really a problem.

I never have anyone hold the horse because it's dangerous for me. If the horse jumps into them, they are going to move out of the way and they are

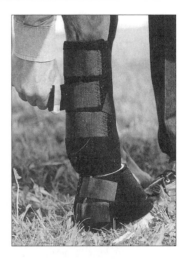

John uses protective boots to prevent horses from hurting their legs if they should bump into the fence.

likely to turn the horse's hindquarters into me. I've found that two scared people around a scared horse ends up in a wreck. (I figure one scared person and one scared horse is enough.)

Seriously, you can't assume that the horse is comfortable with having boots put on. Just take it slow and put in little steps. By going back to the nose each time and taking your time doing this, you are setting up a pattern — letting the horse know you are not looking to scare, hurt or overwhelm him.

Ear-pinning at dinnertime

I have a problem with my horse. She pins her ears when I feed her. Although I've had horses for 13 years, this is my first young horse. When she first started the ear pinning, I blamed it on the grain, then I blamed it on her diet. Then, I blamed it on the adult horses who were next to her and ran in and out during feeding time, pinning their ears. Now, I don't want excuses; I want it to stop.

She'll do anything I ask of her, but she won't quit pinning those ears back. I'm aware of the dangers involved with this behavior. I lost my two front teeth when a mare we'd only had a few days got mad and kicked out when I entered her stall as she was eating.

I don't know what to do. I have taught her to stand quietly three or four feet away from her feeder until I put the food in. She will stand there until I tell her "OK." I do not move away from the feeder until she starts to eat. When I come back in with her pellets, she will back up and wait until I tell her OK again. But her ears are pinned back the whole time. Am I expecting too much of her? Am I too sensitive about this because of my accident?

LW/Norco, CA

You are not being too sensitive; you are just more aware than many people of what can happen, and you recognize the importance of it. And, as you've also recognized, blaming the other horses and finding excuses for the horse's behavior isn't healthy. When we excuse something, we learn to accept it. And anything behavioral we accept, we end up reaping the consequences of (or someone else does if we sell the horse).

You are on the right track in: 1) recognizing that you have a problem — just because you haven't gotten kicked yet doesn't mean you don't have a problem; 2) teaching the foal good manners using cues so you can control her in a safe way.

LYONISM ...

IF YOU THINK YOU'VE PRACTICED ENOUGH, YOU HAVEN'T EVEN STARTED. IF YOU THINK YOU'VE DONE A LOT, YOU HAVEN'T EVEN COME CLOSE. WHEN YOU THINK YOUR HORSE HAS THE IDEA, HE DOESN'T HAVE A CLUE.

A young horse is only a horse who will eventually weigh a lot more than she does now — we should still treat her like a 1,000-pound horse, because she'll be that in time. If she's an ill-mannered baby, she'll be an ill-mannered grown horse, until we change that. It's always better to start teaching good manners when the horse is young, which is what you are trying to do.

Everything is a balancing act — from correcting the horse to loving on her. It's not all "get back away from me" that makes a well-mannered horse. It takes 30 times more instruction to teach the horse what we want her to do, than it does telling the horse she did something wrong. So, teaching this young horse ground manners, leading manners, and picking up her feet — all things we want her to learn anyway — will also help her ear-pinning problem.

Picking up her feet when she doesn't particularly want her feet picked up will also help the ear problem. Teaching her to back up with the halter and on voice commands will actually help the ear problem. Although it seems they are not related, they are, because you are developing more and more control of the horse and getting her in the habit of cooperating with you.

What you are doing is good. You are preventing the horse from becoming obnoxious — bumping into you, and trying to get feed from you as you are putting it in her stall — when you feed her.

You can elaborate on what you've begun with your horse — putting the feed in the bucket, having her wait, then come up — by staying in the stall and brushing the horse and loving on her head and ears while she eats. It shows that you are not in competition with her feed, that you can mess with the horse while she's eating and that you're not going to be taking her feed or pushing her away from her feed.

Having a horse stand back while you dump the feed is good to a point, but it can be aggravating to the horse — like telling a hungry teenager that he has to wait four minutes after dinner is on the table before eating. If each time he came to the table the scene was the same, we could be making one problem worse in trying to solve another one. Keep on the course you're on, but be sure your cues aren't aggravating and you don't ask the horse to wait too long before eating.

Anxious at feeding time

My daughter just bought a four-year-old Quarter Horse off the track. The problem is not in his riding training, but with his dinnertime manners. When it comes time to be fed, he is ridiculous — charging the horse near him, biting the stall bars, and kicking the stall wall. The rest of the time he is a love.

I've tried feeding him first or last, but the problem seems to be when he anticipates being fed. Sometimes he begins to eat and then charges the wall. I'm concerned with my safety when he does this, since I'm not always out of his stall by then.

My daughter wants to put him in leg chains because she doesn't want him to hurt himself kicking. What should we do?

JV/Internet

You have several options. First, when the horse does this behavior, don't yell at him or make a fuss. If you do, you are paying him attention, in effect, rewarding the behavior you don't want.

You can try filling a squirt gun with water and squirt the horse or throw a cup of water on him when he does the behavior you don't want. That may startle him enough that he'll quit it.

You can try turning the horse out in a small paddock at feeding time. Go feed the other horses, then bring the horse in with his feed all ready for him. You'll want to combine this with teaching him great leading manners.

If the horse is becoming aggressive toward people, take care of that through round-pen work and ground manners so that when you open the stall door you can tell him to turn away or toward you, or to stand in a certain place in the stall. Needless to say, you'll want to teach him these things so he's consistent at times other than feeding time, before you ask him to do that at feeding time. Always work from a position of control.

Don't use leg chains. Leg chains and upside-down horseshoes and all that kind of thing that are sometimes used to discourage kicking can end up crippling horses. The object is to solve the behavior problem but end up with a sound horse.

If you want to go to the trouble, you can hang heavy-duty stall mats about 12 inches away from the wall, so when the horse kicks the mat, he doesn't hurt his legs and he doesn't get the satisfaction of hearing himself kick the wall.

Cinchy and nippy

I've tried your lesson for cinchy horses — give a slight squeeze around the girth then quickly release it. When I do this, my horse still moves to nip me. I can do this exercise 100 times and her head will always turn in a negative way toward me. What I am thinking is, if a fly lands on a horse, the horse's reaction is always to turn its head to nip or shoo away the fly. What makes my squeezing around the girth any different from a fly landing on her?

MJD/Wykoff, MN

Your question is logical, but before I give you a solution for your horse's nipping problem, let's follow the line of thinking about the fly irritating the horse. Many people are puzzled about why a horse should accept training of one kind or another.

Everything we do is likely to aggravate the horse, whether it's putting a cinch on or picking up his feet, floating his teeth or giving him deworming medicine. There are many scenarios we can come up with to justify, from the horse's standpoint, his aggravation with us and what we are doing. Carried to an extreme, we could end up justifying not being able to do anything with our horses because what we are asking may be slightly unfair to the horse.

The long and the short of it is that the horse should be safe for us to be around. If the horse is behaving in an unsafe manner, we have to tell him, "Fair or not fair, you do have to tolerate what we are doing."

The cinchy horse problem requires a plan — tighten the girth quickly, then release it quickly before the horse has time to react.

But, at the same time we have to ask ourselves the all-important question, "Are we asking too much of the horse? Is what we are asking of the horse unreasonable?"

Is it unreasonable to ask this horse to tolerate our hand putting slight pressure underneath his stomach? We're not pulling, pinching, stabbing, cutting or hurting the horse. Should he tolerate this without giving us a reaction that is basically dangerous for us and for other people who are around him?

My answer would be, "No, we're not asking too much." Each person has to answer that question themselves. It's not a question that we have to justify to other people; it's a question that the owner has to justify to herself or himself.

There's another aspect to all of this, that is, our horse's welfare. It's a funny way to look at it and sounds far-fetched at first, but the scene happens all too often. If we don't teach the horse to tolerate reasonable aggravations, then he becomes increasingly dangerous. Eventually the horse may hurt somebody, then people start referring to him in a negative way, like saying he's dangerous, or untrainable. Meaning well and not wanting anyone to get hurt, the owners contemplate putting the horse down. So then, because we didn't teach the horse to accept normal handling in life with good manners, the horse ends up in the glue factory.

So, how to solve the problem of the horse nipping? It's a simple, easy-to-solve problem. Put the problem in perspective.

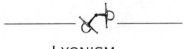

LYONISM ...

PERFORMANCE IS

NEVER LOCKED OUT

BY THE HORSE. IT IS

LOCKED OUT BY AN

INDIVIDUAL PIECE

OF THE HORSE.

While you have your right hand underneath the horse in the girth area, watch the horse's head and mouth area out of the corner of your eye. If she starts to swing her head around toward you, swing your left elbow toward her nose or mouth while the horse is bringing her head toward you to nip, so you actually bump her jawbone with your elbow. But, continue doing what you were doing with your right hand, and act like you didn't do anything.

Act like it was an accident, that the horse did it to herself. As she brought her head around to the side, your elbow happened to be going the opposite direction as her head; so it was a pretty good bump on the jawbone. She'll just have to be more careful next time. Just a few times usually solves the problem.

Treats as rewards

When you are teaching your horse to load into the trailer, do you use food as a reward?

SWT/Internet

No. If the horse goes into the trailer for feed, what happens when he's not hungry, or when something else seems more important to him? I also don't feed treats when training or as a reward when the horse comes to me. If he comes to me because I give him treats and I don't give him a treat one time, I have lied to the horse. I teach the horse to come to me, and always pet him when he does. That way I can always give him the same reward.

Do I let him know I'm scared?

I've heard that you should never let a horse know when you are scared, that he'll take advantage of you. Is that right? My horse already knows that I'm scared of him when I'm leading him. What can I do about that?

KM/Dayton, OH

I consider my horse as my partner, so I never use the "take advantage of" type of language. That would set up an adversarial relationship. Horses don't intentionally take advantage of us, but since they are experts at reading body language, we often send them the wrong signals.

For instance, when a horse moves toward us and we step back, we've allowed the horse to push us around using ordinary dominance language. When horses learn they can dominate another animal or a person, they do. So if you step away because you're afraid, the horse may step forward, maybe even just being nosey or friendly at first. If you step back again, he may move toward you again. He learns that he can move you the way he would move another horse in the field or a cow.

Most horses are scared of cattle when they first see them. But when they learn they can move the cattle, they become more aggressive and move the cattle where they want. They aren't sensing the cow's fear — the cow probably isn't scared — the horse just learns he can push the cow around.

So what do you do about this? First, don't pretend when you are working with a horse. Second, only do what you feel safe doing. Third, use the same dominance language to establish yourself as the head of a two-person herd. Take advantage of the million little opportunities you have when grooming or handling your horse to ask him to cooperate with you. Tell him to move over one step, or back one step. Ask him to move his shoulder over, and when he moves back, tell him to move over again until he stands where you tell him. You can do this even just asking for one step. It's not that you are trying to tell him to go somewhere, like across a creek, that he may not want to go. Instead, you are using ordinary situations to ask him to move a few inches but in the direction that you've chosen. Don't make a big deal about it, just be persistent.

Or you can choose any simple movement and practice it to get the horse in the habit of saying "yes" to your requests. For instance, if you feel safe picking up his front foot, do that 20 times (make sure you're not squeezing his tendon or doing something to cause him pain). After about three times, the horse may think you've done enough of it, but if you stick with it, putting his foot nicely on the ground so he doesn't hit his toe and petting him when each time is over, you'll be developing cooperation.

The WESN (directional control) lesson is particularly good for building handler confidence and a horse's manners, as the exercise is a matter of telling the horse to step forward, step back, step left and right. ▣

21

Dear John: Answers To Your Riding Questions

ontrol problems seem — and often are — more serious when
you are in the saddle than when you are handling the horse
from the ground. But the same control solutions apply in
both cases. We'll look at a variety of riding problems, but
keep the ground-control principles in mind as you read. It will give
you insight into your own training situations.

When you get stuck

I'm writing you because I'm frustrated. I love the gentle, systematic
approach, and I want to be a good teacher to my horse. But, when
partway through the lesson he does something that I didn't expect,
I don't know what to do. Sometimes I think I should scold him,
and other times I think I should reward him because he tried.

GC/Del Mar, CA

You've posed a good question, and it's one many riders struggle
with. I'm often faced with the situation that the horse did something
because he thought it was what I wanted, but I actually wanted him
to do something else. I fall back on some rules of thumb to know
what to do next:

Never scold. Scolding never tells the horse what you want him to
do, and more often than not, scolding results in behavior you don't

81

want. For instance, when you jerk on the reins, his head will go up and he'll be nervous that you'll jerk again.

But I don't always reward him entirely. For instance, if I ask a horse for an inside turn in the round pen and he turns to the outside, I send him back the other direction as quickly as I can. That way I just tell him, "No, not that," without scolding him. Then I ask again. Eventually when an outside turn doesn't work, he'll try an inside turn. Then I'll let him proceed in the new direction. By just saying "Try again," I haven't discouraged him.

LYONISM ...

GO TO THE POINT IN THE TRAINING WHERE YOU CAN GET THE RESPONSE YOU WANT. GET THE RESPONSE CONSISTENTLY, WHICH MEANS ASK AND GET THE RESPONSE YOU WANT SEVERAL TIMES. THEN IMPROVE THE RESPONSE.

If your horse repeatedly gives you a wrong answer to the question you are asking, then you need to find another question. Break your lesson plan down. For instance, if I'm asking for a left-lead canter and he repeatedly steps into the right lead, I'll backtrack and set him up better, or ask for the canter from a long trot or in a place where taking the canter would be easy for him.

Also remember that the horse will go through learning cycles, first seeming to know the right answer, then seeming not to know. He's not being ornery. He'll get the right answer lots of times before he knows exactly what it is that you are asking him. If you change your cue while he's still working it out, then you'll confuse him. If his performance is inconsistent, use the "try again" method.

Learn to look for little improvements, then you won't get discouraged. Also, you'll be quicker to tell the horse when he's doing what you want. That will help him learn.

When all else fails, drop back a few steps in your lesson plan. Practice the step before the one you are having difficulty with, until the horse responds correctly 100 percent of the time. Then increase the excitement level until he can respond 100 percent of the time even when excited. Often, by perfecting the earlier steps in a lesson, the later steps fall into place easier.

Is a snaffle necessary?

I've been riding my horse in a grazing bit, and he responds just fine. I know you recommend a snaffle bit. Is there anything wrong with continuing in the bit I now have?

RG/San Diego, CA

If your horse is doing everything that you want him to do and responding every time you pick up the reins, then there's no need to change what you are doing — and that includes the bit. However, if you want to improve his performance or your control over him, then a snaffle is the training bit that I recommend.

Use my regular bit on trail?

I primarily use my horse for trail riding and have never used anything other than a shank snaffle with a smooth mouthpiece. After beginning work with the full cheek snaffle, I find I just do not feel as confident or sure of control of my horse out on the trail as when I use the shank snaffle, due to the fact that my horse gets excited and, at times, spooky. I do not use the bit for control any more than is necessary because I do not want a hard-mouthed horse. Can satisfactory results be achieved in this training by working him in the full cheek snaffle in these exercises and using my other bit when trail riding?

FB/Rock Hill, SC

Yes. Using the bit frequently, as when you are teaching the horse to give to the bit, does not make the horse hard-mouthed. "Hard mouth" refers to when the horse isn't responding to the bit. It's caused by incorrect use of the bit, not overuse of the bit. The fact that the horse is not responding to the snaffle bit when on the trail tells the rider that they have to practice and get the horse more responsive to the bridle.

You are wise in recognizing that you don't have enough control of your horse, and your solution is a good one for the interim. It's fine to use your regular bit when you are on the trail. But you'll want to work on getting the horse more responsive to the bridle in a confined area where you feel safe, so that the horse will respond the same out on the trail.

Recognize that you may not have the control you think you have with the shank snaffle either. Teaching your horse the "calm down" cue and teaching him to overcome spookiness are important as well as teaching him to give to the snaffle bit. You are on the right track.

Wants a permanent change

I am training a gentle, good-natured, four-year-old Missouri Foxtrotter gelding who had previously been started and ridden using a Tom Thumb bit. Because of the shape of this horse's mouth, this bit left no room for his tongue, so he got in the habit of keeping his tongue on top of it. I put him through your round-pen lessons and started him immediately in a full cheek snaffle.

I began the "giving to the bit" exercises. I thought if I kept him busy, eventually he would forget about messing with the bit. When this didn't seem to work, I tried using a strap tied to the bit and then looped around his nose to hold the bit to the top of the mouth. This kept his tongue under the bit, but it seemed to be such a distraction that it seemed to hinder the "giving to the bit" exercises. I have also tried a dropped noseband and periodically try to go back to the snaffle bit, but his tongue immediately comes over the bit.

No matter how you train your horse, you'll have to continue training him in order for his performance to stay at peak level.

I also tried a horrible-looking broken-type bit with a big spoon in the middle to hold the tongue down. It seemed to work for a while, and I continued successfully his "giving to the bit" exercises. Since he has an agile, long tongue, eventually he discovered he could use the spoon as a wedge to get his tongue over it also. Once his tongue is over the bit, he becomes so distracted that it is difficult to maintain his attention.

In desperation I tried a curb with a high port and a copper roller. This enabled me to get him supple and to teach him to neck rein with little pressure and leg aids, and to halt and back using the raising of the rein and leg and weight aids. He works well for me.

The problem is that I only have him for 45 days and will be turning him over to a relatively inexperienced rider. I am insisting on giving the rider lessons, but I know that this type of bit is easily misused. Can you give me any other ideas on how I might be able to break this habit permanently?

JM/Internet

There is no such thing as a permanent change. Every horse adapts to his circumstances. So the horse's ongoing performance regarding any part of his training, not just carrying the bit, will depend on the rider's consistency with the training. As you instinctively know, changing bits isn't the answer. The quick-fix approach, just switching bits, will result in the horse being out of control, as well as having his tongue over the bit.

Train using the full cheek snaffle, but be sure it is not too low in the horse's mouth. Just ignore the tongue problem and continue teaching the horse to "give," making sure you release the rein completely after each give. Increase the frequency of the gives, so you are asking more of the horse, and rewarding him more often. As you keep his mouth busy, he'll fuss less with the bit, and be learning responsiveness besides.

Ride in a controlled area so you stay safe. Do not ride this horse in a potentially dangerous environment, like on the trail, with his tongue over the bit. If, for safety reasons, you have to use the curb for a time, such as when other horses are in the arena or you are riding outside the arena, then do so, but put the snaffle on to cool the horse out.

Though the tongue problem seems major, the real problem is that the horse is distracted, which means his attention is not on the rider. You'll want to do lots and lots of gives, getting the horse to give with each part of his body, not just his jaw. Also work on speed control, speeding up and slowing down, and asking for changes of direction.

Look for exercises in which you and the horse can get along easily, so he gets in the habit of cooperating. You'll build your horse's emotional control, develop better responsiveness to the bit and your legs, and get him focusing on matters other than his mouth.

A horse, not a bloodhound

I've taught my mare to drop her head in response to the bit, but lately she holds it so low, it's like I'm riding a bloodhound. About half the time she'll carry her head level to her withers, but the rest of the time it's too low. When I try to pick it up, she chomps on the bit and tosses her head. I'm afraid of creating a hard mouth. What should I do?

MH/Linesville, PA

It's a horse's natural tendency to get heavier on the bit when given the opportunity, and she recognizes that when her head is down, she doesn't have any contact with the bit. You'll want to bring her head up the same way you taught her to drop it.

Take the slack out of one rein, and hold it until she begins to bring her head up. Then release the rein. Just as when teaching her to put her head down, or if you taught her to give to the bit, it's likely that she'll toss her head or pull on the rein. That doesn't matter. Just hold the one rein until she does what you want. She'll figure out where the release is and learn to carry her head where you want it.

There's no danger of making her hard-mouthed if you use one rein and release it totally between requests.

Grabs shank

I use my six-year-old gelding in parades, on trails, gathering cattle and roping. He has a bad habit of grabbing the shank of his bit and chewing on it. He tends to only grab the left shank.

It doesn't seem to be a nervous habit because even if we are quietly standing he will grab it and chew on it. I've used a broken snaffle with a copper roller in the middle, a mechanical hackamore, and a D-ring snaffle. In the snaffle, he will work the bit into his teeth and chew on it.

This started when he graduated from the snaffle to a curb style. I would really appreciate any suggestions you may have.

SH/Internet

If a horse is chewing on the bit, it's a sign to the rider that the horse doesn't have enough to do or think about. You'll want to use the replacement concept in dealing with this problem. If the horse is doing something you don't want him to do, ask him to do something you want him to do.

Do not scold the horse to get the bit out of his mouth or yank on the bit. Don't punish the horse for what he is doing, just give him more to do. This is easiest if you are using a full cheek snaffle and working with the horse as we've been describing in the "giving to the bit" lessons.

When we give the horse free time, he chooses what he wants to do. So, can he chew on the bit while he's walking? If yes, then can he chew on it while he walks and gives to the bit? If yes, then can he chew on it while he walks, gives to the bit and steps to the right with his hindquarters? If yes, can he chew on it while he walks, gives to the bit, move his hindquarters to the right and moves his shoulder to the right? Eventually you'll get to a point where he can't do what you are asking him to do and also chew on the bit.

The exercise I just mentioned may not be the one for your horse. Maybe it's flying lead changes or trotting circles, making the circles larger and smaller. But if you use the replacement concept and keep working on his performance, eventually he'll be so busy doing what you want that he'll quit chewing on the bit.

"Baby give" or "calm down"

After getting 3,000 "baby gives" on each rein over several training sessions, I began teaching my horse the "calm down" cue. I understand I have thousands of repetitions of "baby gives" and the "calm down" cue to do before these cues become conditioned responses. But, what is the best mix for practicing these cues? Should it be several training sessions of "baby gives" alternating with several sessions of "calm down"? Should it be half one and half the other in each session?

MS/Killingworth, CT

It should only take one or two sessions of teaching the horse to drop his head all the way to the ground (the "calm down" cue) for him to do it consistently at a standstill or a walk. Once you've taught the cue and the horse knows it, then you don't want to drill it — just use the cue when you get in a situation where you want the horse to calm down.

The cue to "give to the bit" to the side seems to us to be the same cue as the "calm down" cue, but when we focus on the behavior we want, the horse can tell the difference between the two requests.

You'll know the horse has learned the "calm down" cue when you can put a lot of pressure — five, 10 or 15 pounds — on the rein and the horse's head goes down immediately in all situations. The more pressure we put on the rein, the more adamant the horse should get about wanting to put his head down.

The horse may not necessarily drop his head all the way down at once. It may take repeated requests at two second intervals. For instance, on a trail ride with other horses it may take staying focused on that particular exercise for several hours or possibly even the whole trail ride, especially during the first five or six rides. It doesn't take long to teach it, but being able to apply it in different situations or exciting environments will take work for both you and the horse.

Every time we ride, we should work with the horse on the "giving to the bit" lesson, on getting softness of the jawbone and making sure the horse stays soft and responsive with his neck, shoulders and jaw. While giving becomes a conditioned response, getting stiff or leaning on the bit is natural. Quick, light response comes when we keep working on the "baby give."

When other folks ride your horse

I have two horses, and I ride them all the time. I know John says that if you ask the horse to do something and he doesn't, but you (however unintentionally) reward him by releasing the rein, the horse will learn that your signal means nothing. But people who know practically nothing about horses come out and ride my Arab, and they don't want to listen to any instructions. So my question is this: Will my horse know the difference between when I ride her and when other people ride her? Will she still listen to my signals, even if the other riders don't use them?

AMA/Internet

The answer is yes — your horse will recognize the difference between you and the other riders, as long as you are the one riding her most often, and you spend time making sure your signals are consistent. For instance, if you ride her 90 percent of the time, it's really only 10 percent of the time that someone else is giving her different signals. While that won't completely mess her up, it does affect her training, but usually not dramatically. As long as you know they are safe, it's not terrible to let other people go "play" once in a while.

As you know, the horse is always learning, whether it's something we want her to know or not. So, when we release the rein, for instance, when she throws her head, she's learning that we reward her head-tossing.

Horses are extremely adaptable. If you've trained him once, and he's learned something else in the meanwhile, you can always retrain him using the same motivator and reward as you did the first time.

Will riding bareback help?

My husband rode bareback as a kid, and he's nearly fearless when riding now. I am a fairly timid rider, and people have suggested that I ride bareback to develop my seat and confidence. Is this a good idea?

MBR/Valley Forge, PA

The main consideration is how you feel about it. Don't do anything that you don't feel 100 percent safe doing — even if the exercise itself is good. Find something — even if it's just brushing the horse or riding at a walk in the arena — that you are really comfortable

Done in moderation, bareback riding on an easily controlled horse can be both fun and beneficial.

doing, and do that until you get so bored with it or feel confident enough to do something a little more challenging.

Generally speaking, I don't advise timid riders to ride bareback. It's so much more slippery and it's easier to get off balance. Even if you don't fall, you may end up worried about falling.

If you are planning to ride with a saddle, then practice with a saddle. Unless your goal is to ride bareback nearly all the time, I don't think a lot of bareback riding helps you improve your riding skill or even balance.

When you see people who ride bareback most of the time ride with a saddle, they lose their stirrups. That's because they are practiced at gripping the horse with their legs. When you ride with the saddle, your weight goes onto the stirrups and you don't grip.

A little bareback riding at slow speeds can help you learn to feel the horse better, but only if you don't hold on with your legs. Go slowly enough and make your turns wide enough that you can let your legs hang free of the horse. Then your seat really can feel the horse's movements better.

People often ask me about bareback pads. They are fine for cushioning your seat, but they are not as secure as a saddle. If you use a bareback pad, do not use one with stirrups.

Sitting down on the job

About a year ago I purchased a bargain-basement horse who was half-starved. I did this without really knowing anything about him.

I spent the last year rehabilitating Clarence. Now that he's fit, he's revealed dangerous habits. He has good manners when I'm on the ground handling him, but he does not want to be ridden.

His favorite tactic is to sit down with the rider on his back. The first time he did this, I wasn't sure it was deliberate. The second time, he sat down while I was saddling him. I just waited for him to get tired (he was still in cross-ties), and when he got up I continued as if nothing had happened.

The last time Clarence sat down was while my eight-year-old nephew was riding him. Now, I knew I had to show him that he couldn't get out of working just by doing that, so I got on him. He was smart enough to know that the same trick wouldn't work again, so instead he bucked me off. I chased after him and got on again, just long enough to make the dismount be by my choice, not his. As punishment, I left him to spend the rest of the day alone in his stall, separated from my mare.

Fortunately, neither my nephew nor I were seriously injured that day, but I'm not interested in rodeo riding. Can you suggest a safe method for breaking this habit?

MS/Leland, IL

I would consider Clarence an "unbroke" horse. What you tell me indicates that he hasn't learned several basic lessons, which makes it dangerous to proceed as if he's trained.

He isn't trying to get out of being ridden — even though he's been ridden before he is not trained. The fact that we can get on a horse and move him around doesn't indicate that the horse is ready to ride. I wouldn't ride this horse (literally, I wouldn't ride him; I'm not just advising you) before doing a lot of ground work.

Treat him as if he's never been ridden. It sounds as if the horse isn't comfortable with being saddled — which means that he probably hasn't been thoroughly sacked out and saddled correctly.

When a horse sits down on the crossties, that tells me that the horse hasn't been taught to yield to pressure. Do not tie him, or especially crosstie him, until you've taught him to yield to pressure when he feels it on the halter.

Then, go through all the ground and leading lessons with the bridle on. Do quite a bit of work with the horse wearing a bridle instead of a halter, because it will give you better control.

Teach the "giving to the bit" exercises from the ground. Then, making sure all the sacking out, saddling and mounting lessons have been taught, get on the horse and teach the horse to give to the bit while mounted.

Definitely, I would not put any kids on this horse for a long time. The horse is not trying to get out of anything. The only time a horse gets out of anything is when he is doing exactly what the rider wants. It would be a lot easier for this horse to go for a little ride, but he isn't trained to do that.

A natural, but unwanted, reaction

We have been working for about a year with a nearly three-year-old Quarter Horse gelding. My husband and I have had great success with all the techniques in Perfect Horse, *and we've taken our time in the sacking and saddling training. When we started working on "The First Ride," things were going well. So my husband decided it was time to get on.*

Oh, boy. Our calm young horse took off. Since he started from the middle of the round pen, the horse went straight for the gate. He found it shut and took a swift left turn. Unfortunately, my husband took a sharp right to the ground. Though not seriously hurt, he did not get back on. We want to know where to resume the training. We don't want the horse to think that's all he has to do to get someone off permanently.

JF/Burleson, TX

Your horse didn't intentionally do anything to get your husband off; he just got scared and reacted naturally. And ran. He made a legitimate mistake. He definitely wasn't trying to get out of anything.

When a horse is doing what I don't want him to do — in this case, going forward — I ask myself what cue I wish he was responding to instead. If I could put pressure on the rein and have the horse stop, then I'd have a cue that would prevent the horse running away with me. The other thing I could do is to pick up on the rein and have his hip move two big steps to the side — that would prevent him from running forward also.

In this case, I would work from the ground with the bridle on. I would teach the horse to respond to the bridle, so that I could immediately control his hips, or get him to stop with one rein.

I would also repeat the preparation-for-mounting sequence, approaching the horse, petting him, putting a foot in the stirrup, then removing my foot, petting the horse and walking away. I'd do this on both sides, working my way up to getting halfway on the horse with him totally relaxed. If he starts to move forward at any point, just pick up the rein closest to the side you are getting on, hold tension on the rein until he moves his hips over or stops, then release the rein. Proceed with the training that way.

Don't make a big deal about any of this; just matter-of-factly get him more solid in the lessons preliminary to being ridden. That will give you much better control in the saddle, as well.

Discouraged about bucking

I am very discouraged. I had a wreck with my horse two nights ago. I have been trying to use many of the ideas/teaching methods you use, and I was so pleased with her progress. In my back pocket, I had a piece of white paper that I was going to hand to someone on the ground. I knew the mare might be afraid of this, so I moved slowly to hand the paper down. She bolted. I attempted to stop her with the snaffle bit, but I reacted first by pulling straight back. Before I could pull left or right, she started some serious bucking, and I was thrown off.

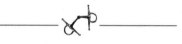

LYONISM ...

THE NEATEST THING ABOUT LEARNING TO GIVE TO THE BIT IS THAT THE HORSE CAN GIVE TO THE BIT WITH ANY SPOT ON HIS BODY.

My greatest concern is: Did she buck out of fear? I am sure I squeezed her with my legs when she bolted, which may have scared her more. Or was the bucking out of meanness? I have worked with her on the ground with some spooky things, including paper. I did get back on her after the wreck, and she was calm. I did not scold her, but we did some circles. Please give me your thoughts about what to do. This mare had come a long way. I understand why she bolted, but I am not sure why she bucked.

TA/Internet

Actually the whole situation is pretty positive in that neither you nor the horse were seriously hurt. And there is a lot that we can learn from your experience. The horse just got scared. You did the right thing in not scolding her.

It was fine that you got back on the horse, but it wouldn't have been a priority. In those cases you should only get on if you know you will be safe and the horse will be under control. The horse would not have gotten away with anything if you had not ridden her again that day.

What can you learn from this experience? The most important thing is that you are really a better trainer than you may think. That little voice inside warned you — you suspected on the front end that handling the paper might make her nervous — so you really had the information you needed. If we're not sure we'll be safe if we do thus and so, that's the voice of common sense.

If you had followed your instincts and stepped down from the horse to hand the paper to someone else, the wreck would probably have been averted. You would also have thought to yourself, "I really don't want to have to get off my horse every time. I'd better do more work with her so I can be safe doing things while I'm still in the saddle." So you were on the right track; you just overstepped that caution.

I tell people to ask themselves if they'll be safe doing something — for instance, getting on a green horse for the first time. If they say "probably," I tell them that probably isn't good enough. You were lucky in that no one was hurt — and lots of other people are lucky some of the time. We don't want to trust our safety to luck, however, but to solid training instead.

Next you learned that your horse didn't obey your rein signals to stop. It doesn't matter whether you used one rein or two — the horse didn't respond at a gallop. That raises two matters of training. First, you must train the horse to respond to the rein. I'd do lots of giving to the bit, using the rein to get the horse to move her hips over and so forth.

The other consideration is speed. Your horse may give to the bit well or respond great at the walk or trot, but how many times have you asked her to stop at a dead run? (Sounds like she isn't far enough in her training to be doing that, but we're looking ahead.) We can't expect a horse to stop at a dead run if we've never trained him to do that. So once she's responding well to the reins, then you'll want to add the speed factor to your training. In a safe environment, practice stopping at the walk, then at the trot and so forth, until you can stop at a gallop.

A slow walker

I'm tired of riding a horse who is pokey at the walk. But when I ask him to speed up, he goes into a trot or lope. How can I get him to walk faster?

TM/Internet

You'll want to develop a cue that tells the horse to speed up, not just go into another gait. The cue that works best for most people is to bump the horse with both of your legs until the horse speeds up, then stop bumping.

If you are doing this in the walk, you may have to be prepared to bump for quite a while if the horse isn't responsive, which is why it's easier to teach this cue in the trot. Just keep bumping, which will irritate the horse, even if he doesn't register irritation. Then end the irritation as soon as the horse speeds up.

Work at the trot, doing exercises speeding the horse up and slowing him down again. Then go back to a walk. When you give the horse the same cue to speed up in the walk, he'll have a tendency to walk faster instead of going into the trot.

If the horse breaks into a trot, bring him back to a walk and ride "faster," allowing your seat and body to move with the horse.

A horse learns to walk at the speed required of him.

Personality or training?

My 10-year-old Quarter Horse gelding is calm and sensible most of the time. He has good ground manners and will stand for bathing, clipping, grooming and shoeing. He seems to like and trust people. He's a good trail horse, doesn't spook a lot and goes where you ask him to as long as we're just walking or trotting.

The problem is that he gets excited in new places and even in old ones when there are other people and horses running around. He will buck, and if you try to hold him back, he will throw his head. If you let him go with the other horses, he will still buck.

He's sluggish in the arena, and it's even hard to get him to lope. He's out with three other geldings during the day and stalled at night. Is this just his personality, or is there some way to get him over this?

JH/Coos Bay, OR

It's not a personality problem, nor is it unusual. In fact, many horses who buck follow the same pattern. What you'll want to do is get your horse more responsive to your cues in calm settings so that he can respond to them when he's excited.

First, get your horse less lethargic at home by practicing trotting, then extending the trot. We call that "working the gas pedal." Practice starting and stopping until you have him under good control.

You need a specific cue to tell him to speed up. Leaning forward, releasing the reins or kissing to the horse are not adequate. Start by kicking him lightly and rhythmically with both legs. Keep kicking until he moves forward. You want a noticeable change in leg speed. You are setting him up to learn the cue that when you kick him with both legs, he should increase his leg speed or you'll keep kicking him — no matter how long it takes. Sooner or later, the horse will speed up even just a few steps. Immediately stop kicking.

Then you should ask him to slow down before he slows down on his own, even if it's just 20 strides after you got him moving. That way he knows you are not going to ask him to go fast for too long. When you work with this, you'll be practicing both the "speed up" and the "slow down" cues.

Since the problem happens when the horse gets excited, practice control in calm, but then in exciting situations. Speed is always exciting to a horse, so you can ask him to trot, then trot fast, then walk, then immediately trot again. By shortening the time between the things you ask the horse to do, you can get him excited. Through the course of different trotting speeds, changes of direction, inside the arena, out in an empty pasture and so forth, you can do lots to teach the horse good control before you ask him to lope. Be sure that you've taught your horse the "calm down" cue so that you have a specific cue to tell him to relax when he gets too excited.

Once you have good control at the trot, then practice the same kinds of exercises loping in controlled environments, and build up his speed.

When you are on the trail with other horses, ride with them, then away from them, using the buddy sour-type lessons.

After all that, when you are next in a situation where you think he's going to begin shaking his head, put him to work practicing one of the cues that he does best at home. Ask him to do one thing, like moving his hips over, then immediately ask him to do something else, like turning one way, stopping a moment, trotting, then walking and so forth. The idea is to do exercises in rapid-fire succession, so he has to stay thinking about your signals and not whatever else is going on.

No matter what he does, don't you lose your focus. Just concentrate on what you are asking him to do rather than reacting to what he's doing.

Try not to ask him to stand still when he's on the trail, especially when the other horses are doing something else. That only stresses the situation. It would be fine to do as a "final exam," once you're sure the horse has finished the course of lessons, but not before then.

Loping for the first time

About a year ago, my three-year-old mare and I had an accident that left me a little afraid. She reared. I fell off, and she tripped backward on top of me. After that, we went back to basic training.

My problem is that she no longer wants to work in the round pen. I take her out with other horses and ride in the pasture. She responds to leg cues, she stops and turns, but she is somewhat of a free spirit and difficult to control when she leaves one horse at home. I am afraid of loping her in the pasture and having her run away.

I have trotted her in circles at the town arena, but I really want to lope her first in the round pen. But she stops, humps up and will not respond to my cues when I ride her in the pen. I wear myself out kicking her forward. Out of the round pen she moves faster than I want her to. What should I do?

CL/Internet

Controlling a horse's hindquarters is important at the lope — for both basic control and later on for more advanced maneuvers, like lead changes.

You have mentioned several problems, all of which involve lack of control. Your horse is telling you that she isn't in your control in the round pen (not going forward is as out of control as not stopping). In the pasture, she's probably paying more attention to the other horses than to you, and the town arena is probably not safe if any major distraction occurred. If I couldn't ride in a small, familiar pen, then I know I wouldn't feel safe in a larger area where there are situations or distractions beyond my control. Going back to basics in a small enclosure or round pen is the right thing.

Before discussing loping, let's talk about getting the horse to move forward on your cue. There are several ways to do this, and several that are probably not safe to try right off.

I would not ride her with other horses until I developed better control. I would not use a riding crop or spurs or have another rider help me get her moving faster. Eventually you'll want your horse to respond to the "speed up" cue. When a horse knows the cue, he knows you'll bump him with both your legs from now until doomsday or until he gives you a noticeable change in leg speed.

But, because you've said that your horse humps up, and because green horses who lock-up often explode when they finally move forward, that's not the place where I'd start with this mare. I'd teach her to move her feet using a bridle cue, which is actually more demanding than using your legs, but much safer.

I'd use the rein to tell her feet to move. Take all the slack out of one rein. Hold that rein immovable until the horse moves her head to the same side. When she does, release the rein. As you keep getting her to move her head to the side, she'll eventually move the front foot on that side, too, to "follow" her nose. Then you can ask for the other foot. This system has the advantage that you are training the horse to give to the bit, as well as "connecting" the rein to her front feet.

Once she gives to the side with her nose, then you can graduate her to "giving" with her front foot. So, instead of releasing the rein when she moves her nose to the side, don't release until she moves her foot. After a few times, she will recognize the pattern that when you pick up one rein while thinking about the front foot on the same side, she's to move it.

Another approach is to "connect" the rein to the hip, taking slack out of one rein (say, the left) as you think about the horse's left hip moving to the right. Keep tension on that one rein until the horse steps over with her hindquarters. Then release the rein. Once her hindquarters move, the front feet will move, too. This has the advantage of giving you a way to control the horse if she gets going too fast — just ask her hips to move over. You can use both systems — connect the rein to the front feet and then to the hindquarters. With repetition, the horse will be able to differentiate what you want, even though to you it may seem like the same signal.

It's extremely important to use good judgment. If you are worried that the horse will buck or rear, teach her the lesson from the ground. That's what I'd do. I do not ride horses who buck or rear. There's always a safer way to work with them. The safer way would be to teach the horse the "go forward" cue from the ground, and teach her to "give to the bit" from the ground also.

I wouldn't worry about the buddy-sour problem until after you get your mare under better control.

Your own fear is actually a good thing. Fear is only common sense in disguise. If you are not in control of the horse you are riding, you should be afraid. That's what keeps you safe.

You shouldn't lope this horse, even after you've taught her to go forward, until you are 100 percent sure that she will be in control when you do ask her to lope. Loping her in the pasture —and particularly with other horses in there — is extremely dangerous until you have very good control.

Drain pipe dragons

I am neither a trainer nor an accomplished rider — just an individual who enjoys trail riding for fun and relaxation. I learned to ride when I was 38, and I bought a 16-year-old gelding who knew everything. We've spent 12 years enjoying riding on trails in good weather and on back roads in bad.

Now he's retired, and I've bought a four-year-old mare. I soon realized I should not have bought a green horse. I sent her to a trainer who started her in the Lyons' method, and I've been working with her and am pleased with how we are progressing, but we aren't yet the perfect horse and rider.

I've thoroughly sacked out my horse using the lessons in Perfect Horse. *She is perfect in her paddock — she ignores balloons, umbrellas, jingle bells, flapping tarps; she'll walk across tarps, wooden ramps, tractor tires and puddles. She lets me rub her all over with plastic bags, feed bags, balloons and stuffed toys. While she's been successfully "spook proofed" at home, what do we do about garbage bags and bicycles on the road? Things she ignores at home still spook her on the road.*

Her biggest fear is the large drain pipes that run along the road to divert water under driveways. My horse seems frightened of the big, gaping drain holes. She wants to make a wide circle around them, which is dangerous should a car be approaching. Additionally, I can't help wondering why the horse would be so frightened of the stationary drains, while the cars that speed by at 40 mph don't faze her.

She gives nicely to the bit in most situations, but these drain-pipe dragons are the exception.

EL/Hopewell, NJ

First, I want to compliment you on the work you've done at home with your horse, teaching her to ignore distractions. You've made a lot of thoughtful steps before going on the trail. When you talk about the horse being comfortable with things at home, we assume you are referring to riding your horse amidst these distractions — not just handling her on the ground.

You can't ask a horse to not be afraid of something. You can only work with her and deal with the fear that she has. The drain pipe really just represents a distraction from your cues to turn left and right — a pop quiz: "Will you respond to this cue, that I think I have taught you, with this level of a distraction going on?"

When you are on the street and the horse moves off to the left, say, away from the drain pipe on the right, use your rein — to tell her to move right — either by using the right rein to tell the right shoulder to go to the right or the left rein to tell the left shoulder to go to the right.

If the horse doesn't respond to this turn-right cue 20 feet from the drain, then go farther down the street, away from the drain, and practice that cue until the horse is consistently turning to the right, say, 30 feet from the drain pipe.

Comparing the car to the drain pipe, the car represents a level-three distraction to this horse. And, at a level-three distraction, she responds well to your cue to turn right. The drain pipe may represent a level-eight distraction. Somewhere in between level three and eight, the horse isn't responding. So we actually need to remove the distraction, which we can do by moving farther from the drain pipe, and keep working until the horse responds consistently at 30 feet. Then, I'd start working her on the cue, closer and closer to the level-eight distraction.

Why the horse picks particular things to be afraid of is really not important. And the drain pipe is not really a bad thing: It provides us an opportunity to test how well we've taught our individual cues at home.

If I had spent an hour or two in the area of the drain pipe teaching the horse to turn left and right, when I got back home, I'd tell myself that my expectations for the horse's response to my cues had not been high enough. If I've been satisfied with her turning within three or four steps or within several seconds of my request, I should be asking her to respond more quickly and be better at the exercise at home.

For instance, if previous to this experience you were satisfied with putting two or three pounds of pressure on the rein to get her to turn, you should increase the level of performance that you want — train her to turn on a half-pound of pressure and to turn quicker. By raising your expectations, you'll end up with a horse who is more responsive to your cues. Then, when you are on the trail and you run across a distraction, she'll respond to your cues despite the distraction.

Relax and ride?

Your articles frequently talk of having mini-lessons as you go down the trail. If I'm riding a horse who is well-behaved, I frequently

Despite their different riding objectives, John and Susie still enjoy exploring the trail together.

relax, talk with friends and don't work on anything. Are you always training, or do you sometimes just let the horse stretch his neck and relax, assuming he behaves well?

RD/Internet

There's no one right way. You can do either, assuming that the horse is well-trained and you don't have to worry about control.

Personally, I'm always working on something. Imagine that you had a great sports car, and that you really enjoy its great handling and performance. That's how I am with Zip and Seattle — I really get into working on performance. So, when I'm training on the trail, I'm having fun — it doesn't feel like work. But, when I'm riding someone else's horse and not thinking training, I can drop the reins and focus on the scenery or the company.

But the focus on training can cause problems, too, for instance when you ride with someone who has a different style. My wife, Susie, can ride her horse, BJ, down almost any trail using just a neck rope — and she rarely even touches that neck rope. When we trail-ride together, she wants to chat and just enjoy time together, and she wishes I'd drop the reins and forget about training. I do that from time to time, but I also realize that when I pick up on the rein with a performance horse, if he doesn't respond correctly and I inadvertently release the rein, I may be compromising his performance. The decision to relax on the trail or train on a well-trained horse is really a matter of personal preference; the horse is versatile enough to do either — or both. ▣

22

My Horse Won't ...

*... those are the three words most commonly used
to begin most reader letters. John shows you
how to change them into "my horse will ..."*

Pretend that you are a first-time rider. You know absolutely
nothing about how to ride. You are sitting happily on your
horse, stirrups adjusted. Now what? You'd most likely ask,
"How to do I get this horse to move?" That would be a logical question for novices to ask, but it's a valid one for experienced
riders to ask, too. In fact, they should pause to think about it, rather
than presume that they know the answer.

If your background was from riding mechanical horses outside
dime stores, you'd automatically look for the coin slot. If you were
a seasoned trail rider, you might release the reins, lean forward, kick
the horse or make kissing noises to tell your horse to go forward.
But when you are "out of quarters" — when your trail horse does-
n't go forward from those signals — what do you have to fall back
on? You need the equivalent of a coin slot for your horse — a conditioned response to a specific cue (your coin).

"But John," you say, "my horse obeys me fine until (fill in the
blank — he sees the cows, he gets left behind, he's scared approaching the creek or bridge)." Your comment would be a natural one, but as we become better horsemen, we realize that the
bridge, cows or other horses are just distractions — not the causes of our horse's behavior. Bottom line is that when our horse isn't
doing what we want, we have to ask ourselves, "What cue do I
wish he was responding to?" Then we can develop a path to gain,
or regain, control.

One of the secrets to having a confident horse is to work him at various speeds, alone and with other horses, and in various locations. Then he'll develop the emotional stability to respond to your cues despite distractions.

Move forward or speed up

If I asked 10 riders how they get their horses moving, I may get 10 answers, some of which are: use your legs, kick him, lean forward and kiss to him, try to turn him and kick at the same time. But what does "use your leg" really mean? A cue has to be really specific.

The cue I use is the gentle bumping of both my legs against the horse's sides. You can use whatever part of your leg is easiest —just the lower leg or the whole leg — but the key will be to continue bumping until the horse gives you a noticeable change in leg speed. That could be from a stop to a walk or from a walk to a fast walk. As soon as the horse's leg speed increases, then I stop bumping.

If I bump and nothing happens, then I keep on bumping. That may sound obvious, but most people approach getting their horse moving the way they would try to start a car with a battery problem — in spurts. They crank for a while, then pause when they are tired of cranking. If we do that when we're riding the horse, we've told him that our cranking — in this case the bumping of our legs — doesn't mean he has to do anything. So instead of it signaling to our horse, it confuses him, and we end up acting in frustration rather than trying to communicate.

Instead, continue bumping with just enough intensity that it will irritate the horse. Most horses will step forward when slightly irritated. Continue bumping until that happens, if he was stopped, or until he increases leg speed if he was walking or trotting. Then immediately let your legs rest quietly, so that the horse feels a reward for his effort.

If you have a hard time getting your horse moving from just standing, practice when you are walking, bumping to go from slow walk to fast walk. If you bump him while you are walking and he goes into a trot, do not pull him back right away. He's done exactly what you wanted — increased leg speed. With time and repetition, you will smooth out your signals, and he'll give you the correct amount of increase, but initially you want only a noticeable change in leg speed.

The rule we keep in mind is: First get the transition you want. Then get the transition consistently. Then get it correctly, then consistently correct. So we want a noticeable change in leg speed once. Then we want to repeat that mini-lesson enough times that each time we begin bumping, our horse gives us an increase in leg speed (that's "consistently"). Once we're absolutely sure that he knows what the cue means — that he hasn't just lucked into doing the right thing a few times — then we'll begin to refine it so that we get the correct transition. Then, as the pattern goes, we'll get that correct transition consistently. Until we have that last part under our belt, we won't consider that the horse has learned the cue.

But let's say that instead of just bumping your horse with your legs, you decide that you are going to outright kick him. If he doesn't increase his leg speed, you'll have to keep on kicking with the same intensity and rhythm that you began, which is really tiring for you and painful for the horse. While you can choose any cue that you want, it's best to choose a cue that is easy and natural for you and not excessively irritating to the horse. Better to teach him to respond to a quiet signal than a "shouted" one.

So let's say that you are bumping away and he's just plugging along at the same speed. You have to tell yourself (and him, with your actions) that you are going to keep bumping from now until forever, or until he speeds up his legs, whichever comes first. At first it may feel like forever will come first, but if you keep your cool and keep bumping, eventually your horse will make a move you can reward.

What happens if, instead of speeding up, he slows down? Keep bumping. If you stop bumping, you'll have taught him that when you bump with your legs, you want him to slow down. (See the logic here?) Whatever the horse does immediately before you reward him will register as the action you want. Or let's say he's standing still and you are kicking away, then he backs up and you stop kicking. You've shown him the new back-up cue.

You can use this same technique in any gait. If he's trotting too slow, bump, bump, bump until he's trotting faster. Then stop bumping. So now we know we can answer the question, "How do I get this horse to move?"

Control with the rein

What if your horse is really slow or just stands still? The "bumping" method doesn't seem to be working. What else can you do? Use your rein. Rein cues are always stronger than leg cues, and we use them as our primary or basic-control cues. Once we've used the rein to get the horse's feet moving, then we can go back to the bump method.

Pick up one rein, taking all the slack out of it, and hold slight tension on the rein until the hip on that side moves over. So if you are holding the left rein, you want the left hip to move to the right. If you keep holding, the horse's neck will tire and he'll want to straighten it out, and he'll probably move his hind end in order to do so. When he moves his hip, release the rein.

You can practice that until every time you pick up that rein, thinking about him moving the left hip, he steps over. With practice, you condition his response to your rein cue. (Of course, you'll have to teach each side separately. The horse doesn't transfer what he learned on one side to the opposite side.)

Once you've developed the ability to move the horse's hips over, then, at a later point, you can use the same tool to slow him down. When he's heading north too fast, for instance, you can tell his hips to move east, then east again, and again, until he slows down or is heading south. If he's now heading south too fast, keep moving his hips over. By moving his hips to the side, the horse loses forward-motion power, and by using a series of direction changes, you can get him under control.

Now that we've figured out how to get the horse moving and stopping, what else can we do with rein cues? Obviously, we can steer, which is really important. We can do this by pointing the horse's nose in a direction, and then telling the horse to move forward. If his neck is relaxed, his toes will point the same direction his nose does.

But when we're in one of the situations we first talked about, the horse's neck is rarely relaxed. When he's scared or refusing to do something, his head is up, his neck is stiffened, and he's ready to

"Connecting the rein to the hip" (which is the same as "giving to the bit" with the hip) requires that the rider pick up the rein while thinking about the horse's hip. Here John actually puts his left hand on Zip's left hip just to emphasize a point for the camera. Zip has started to move that hip, and John is a split second from releasing the rein.

get out of Dodge (which is generally not where you want him to go). We can teach our horse to calm down using a rein cue.

The next step is to tell the horse to drop his head and relax. When his head is elevated, he's in prepare-to-flee mode. For some reason, when we can get the horse to drop his head, he also relaxes, which makes him much easier to control. Like everything we do with our horse, we need a cue. There are lots of subtle cues we can use to tell our horse to relax — a soothing voice, petting, relaxing our seat in the saddle — but none of those are strong enough cues to motivate him to mellow out. We need a strong cue — a rein cue.

Just as we developed a cue to tell the horse to move his hip, we can use the same rein to tell the horse to drop his head ("calm down" cue). We pick up the one rein the same way (you may not have to shorten it as much as for the hip), hold contact with it until you see the tip of his ear drop about a half-inch. Then release the rein. With practice, you can condition the horse to drop his head when you pick up the rein while thinking about him dropping his head.

Keeping him going

By the way, did you know that there's no such thing as a "don't slow down" cue? You can't kick your horse to tell him to keep going without destroying your "speed up" cue.

If you periodically bump him without getting an increase in leg speed, you'll "burn your cue." Instead, if you anticipate that your horse is about to slow down, speed him up and then bring him back to the speed you want.

Three parts of the horse

Now we've developed a cue to tell the horse to go and one to tell him to drop his head. We can tell the physical parts of the horse what to do. But, is getting more specific in our cues going to do the trick for us and our non-bridge-crossing, scared-of-cows, left-behind horse? No. It's a help, but if we are going to really control our horse in difficult situations, we'll have to train all three parts of him —

the physical, mental and emotional aspects.

As we ride our horse and train on him, he gets physically stronger. We only ride a green or out-of-shape horse for a few minutes at first, until he builds up enough strength to be able to go for longer times. We want his muscles to build up so he doesn't come back from a ride sore. We want his tendons,

Here John is again asking Zip's hip to step over, but you can see that he's asking for more advanced performance — Zip's neck is soft, and he's actually stepping diagonally.

ligaments and bones to be strong so he stays sound. And we want to strengthen his cardiovascular system so that he doesn't get out of breath too easily. Training a horse physically isn't much different from training a human athlete.

Then there's the mental aspect. That's where cues and repetition come in. When we train for a conditioned response, we program the horse so that when he recognizes a certain signal, he automatically responds — even if there's a scary bridge ahead. He doesn't even have to think about it. We drop a quarter into the box, and the horsie starts moving. The reason that he knows the difference between when you pick up the rein and want him to move his hips and when you pick up the same rein wanting him to drop his head, is he's learned that when you think about one thing, you are somehow different to him than when you think about something else. We can't quite determine what the difference is, but the horse stores it away in his memory banks. The more cues you teach and the better you teach them, the smarter he seems to become. That's the mental part of the horse at work.

A very fit horse who knows a lot of cues can become totally out of control when he is scared, excited or in pain. Why? Because emotions override his recognition of your cues. So just as people learn to function in emotionally demanding situations, our horse must be so well-conditioned to our cues that he can obey us, despite distractions. Those are the key words — despite distractions. So back to our initial question: "How do I get my horse to ... (cross the bridge, go past the cows, calm down when the other horses leave) despite the distraction of the bridge, cows or other horses?" We have to use the cues we've taught, but we must also train the horse's emotions.

Emotional training

When we think of someone working out in a gym, lifting weights, for instance, we picture them exposing their muscles to a simple demand, then giving them time to relax before another lift. When we train our horse's emotional "muscles," we do the same. We expose them to a small excitement, then ask them to calm down before repeating a small excitement. But just "flexing emotional muscles" won't give us control. We want the horse to obey our cue despite the excitement.

Developing emotional control and responsiveness to rider cues is probably to the horse a little like learning to drive in traffic is to a person. The first time out on the road, each maneuver requires concentration. As the course goes on, the number of turns per lesson increases; the speed of the vehicle increases, and the student is asked to keep cool despite traffic.

Begin with just one lesson — for instance, dropping the head — and practice that at various speeds. When the horse does it well at the walk, begin trotting, then ask him to drop his head. When he does it well at the trot, try the canter.

"Drop his head at the canter?" you say. Yes. If a horse is excited and deciding he's going to head for home, he's likely to take off at a canter. If you've only practiced cues at the walk and trot, you don't have a cue when you really need it.

Then you can take him to a more exciting environment. Ride him up and down the driveway, asking him to drop his head when it gets higher than you want. When he's super responsive there, then head out to an empty pasture, then ride in the pasture with one other rider, and so forth.

Build stimulation and speed in stages, making sure to not challenge the horse beyond where he can respond correctly to your signals. Your goal is to have him answer every request correctly. If he's making mistakes, you're going too fast.

Another way to increase the intensity or excitement is to shorten the time between requests. For instance, "Please do this. Good. Now do that. Good. Now do this." Imagine yourself working at a fast-food restaurant. The tasks are not each hard, but they come along pretty fast and you can find it pretty intense to learn. You want to be sure that he does each request and that you reward each right move, but then ask for something else.

Now you've taught your horse specific cues. You've trained the three facets of him. You are ready to head out to the trail.

On location

The rule we follow is: Ride where you can, not where you can't. That means, if you have great control of your horse when riding alone in the arena, that's where you begin your lesson.

So let's say that you are riding along on the trail. You've taught your horse the cues we've discussed, but he gets a whiff of cows and he's thinking of heading for home. What to do? Where did you have great control of the horse? 60 feet back? 100 yards back? A half-mile back? That's where you begin the "cow" lesson — where the horse is comfortable and has enough emotional discipline that he can obey your cues consistently.

Break it into mini-lessons

What stallion doesn't want to ignore his rider and hob-nob with horses along a fence line? Before they approach the

horses, John gets Zip involved in a mini-lesson, so that his focus is on John and not the horses. That keeps Zip under John's control.

John is working on diagonals — asking Zip to step out at about a 45-degree angle. Notice him stepping to his left in this photo and to the right in the photo below.

As he moves down the fence line, John quietly keeps Zip's focus on the lesson. John already trained Zip to do this movement well in a quiet setting, but training the emotional part of the horse requires practicing cues in potentially more exciting circumstances.

The important part about teaching horses to go away from each other without getting excited is the number of times you separate them, not the distance or time separated.

For the sake of discussion, let's say that your starting place for the "cow" lesson is 100 yards from the cow pasture. Begin working on a familiar exercise right there. Let him know that he's OK — you are just working on training. Choose an exercise that he does exceptionally well at home, for instance, making figure eights.

Figure eight at the walk until he's 100 percent responsive — you'd win the figure eight class if there were one. Then add excitement as we discussed earlier. When he's 100 percent responsive at a faster gait or more exciting situation, allow your figure eight to come two yards closer to the cows, then retreat back. Work at the 98-yard distance until you've got great response there, then move to 95 yards for a few strides. Work the pattern, returning to the "safe" location frequently. Eventually, you can work your way closer until you can ride past the cows, continuing the exercise in a relaxed manner.

It doesn't do any good to force a horse past the cows. Not only doesn't it solve the problem, it further scares the horse, reinforcing in his mind that he shouldn't have gotten so close to the cows. It puts you in an out-of-control or limited-control situation, which is not safe. And the horse only has practice approaching the cows once. We want to give him lots of practice, so he's comfortable and safe to ride the next time we ride past the cows.

By approaching the lesson in the way we've suggested, several things automatically happen:

■ Your concentration, riding skill and timing improve.

■ The horse's responsiveness to all the cues you use for the figure eight improves.

■ The horse learns that he can get worried about cows, but that you are not going to put him in a situation that overfaces him.

■ The horse's confidence in your leadership increases.

■ The cows become less important as the horse increasingly focuses on responding to your cues.

■ As the cows become less important, they become less scary.

The same principle applies to crossing a bridge. Practice your cues a comfortable distance from the bridge, then work your way closer, asking the horse to repeatedly go back to safe territory. You might consider practicing having the horse walk onto unfamiliar surfaces

If a horse is scared or unsure of himself, don't criticize him, but instead help him over his fear. John takes time to make sure this horse doesn't feel rushed or frightened before asking him to cross this concrete bridge. Prior to now, John has made sure that the horse responds well to cues even when excited, because a wreck on a bridge like this could be far more dangerous than an upset in an open field.

in a safe area, like an arena first. When he can walk across a tarp, then graduate to a tarp out in the pasture, then perhaps a sturdy piece of plywood on the ground, and so forth.

What about the horse who gets upset when his buddies leave? He doesn't need time away from his buddies; he needs practice actually separating. So ride together, then separate for 10 feet, then come back together again. Work the same training principles as you increase the distance between buddies.

Once you have worked through this pattern of training with one or two problems, you'll find that you can apply it in many circumstances. Determine what cue you want your horse to respond to. Teach that cue to all three parts of the horse — the physical, mental and emotional. Then ride where you can, not where you can't. Pretty soon, you'll be using the words, "My horse will." PH

23

Dear John:
Answers To Your
Health Care Questions

Some of the best-read parts of *Perfect Horse* magazine are the veterinary questions in Dear John. Our veterinary editor, Dr. Eleanor Kellon, answers reader questions. We've assembled some of the most interesting and helpful.

Eggs for breakfast, anyone?

My name is Cinnamon. I am a five-year-old Fox Trotter in excellent health. My coat really shines. I think it might be because of the three or four eggs I eat daily (with the shell). I have been enjoying this treat for about six months. If this doesn't hurt me, I would like to continue having my treats from the chickens. My boss, Lori, thinks it's too many eggs. What do you think?

Cinnamon/Ask Down, AR

You probably know you are unusual in your tastes, but eggs are just fine. The shell is a rich calcium source, the whites are an excellent source of protein, and the yolk supplies necessary fats.

The only drawback is an enzyme in the raw egg that destroys the B vitamin thiamine. If you are going to make this a regular habit, you should be taking a thiamine supplement, about 60 mg a day, not at the same time as the eggs. There are both liquid and powder thiamine supplements available from any tack shop/supply catalog.

Salmonella contamination of eggs is a concern, too. However, most people and animals are exposed on a regular basis to Salmonella and if their stomach is healthy (normal acid production), the bacteria is killed. If your eggs come from chickens on your own farm or ranch, it is probably not a big concern. If not, Salmonella infection from a particularly hardy strain will be a risk.

Both the thiamine problem and Salmonella infection can be avoided by cooking the eggs. Have you tried them hard-boiled?

Older horses and choke

I have a 23-year-old Quarter Horse gelding, who I Love dearly, who recently had trouble with allergies, heaves and choking. I was nearly at wit's end when I happened to read somewhere that some older horses have difficulty producing enough saliva! My other old horse is a slobbery pig, but Marty... well, I honestly never saw him "slobber"... a light bulb went on immediately!

Before I continue, allow me to share some background on Marty. I bought him just before his 20th birthday and in good health, though just that past winter he and the whole herd from his stable had gone through strangles.

This past winter and spring, however, symptoms of heaves and allergies flared up, and I thought this precipitated his choking episodes. Several vets checked him (I was sure he had some scar tissue build-up in his esophagus from the strangles) and had extensive dental work performed. Several hundred dollars later, his heaves symptoms lessened with the help of medication and wetted hay (senior pelleted food was definitely out for Marty; he choked worse on pellets), but the choking continued despite adding rocks to his bucket to slow him from bolting his feed. I finally resorted to feeding him partial amounts — I had to slow him down.

The next feeding time, I added warm water to Marty's feed (just enough to cover the amount in the scoop), and to this day (about two weeks later) he has not choked once! Perhaps another reader out there may be experiencing the same thing and could benefit from my experience with Marty.

JJS/Internet

The fact your horse didn't choke when eating the wet feed is good evidence that he was not sending enough saliva along with this food. This can be caused, as you said, by a decreased saliva production

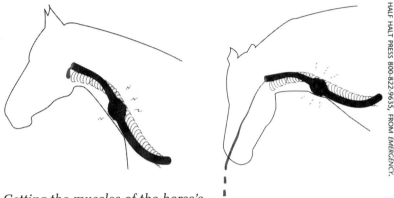

Getting the muscles of the horse's lower neck or throat to relax is extremely important in relieving choke. A horse with choke should be kept relaxed and his head lowered, if possible.

in general, but it is also a common problem with horses like your Marty who eat their feed fast. Chewing is what stimulates the flow of saliva, and chow bolters don't take much time to chew.

Another possibility with Marty is that he still had some swollen lymph tissue in the area of his throat that made swallowing difficult (he may have been more gagging than real "choke"). The moistened feed would be less irritating.

However, wet feed won't work for all horses who choke. Some older horses actually have sections of their esophagus where the nerves don't function properly. Softening the feed might actually make the horse eat it faster (easier to eat) and pack too much into his esophagus at one time. Experts disagree on what's best for a horse who chokes for this reason, but wet feeds that are more like a soup seem to be handled the best.

Just a few words about choke: When you or I are choking, it means we have food stuck in our windpipe (trachea). "Choke" in horses refers to something different. It is when food becomes stuck or packed into the esophagus — the tube between his mouth and his stomach.

The horse will stand with his head low and neck extended forward. Saliva drips from his mouth because it cannot get past the obstruction. If you suspect choke, call the vet right away. This is an emergency. Unless the blockage is relieved quickly, the esophagus can be damaged or even ruptured.

Put the horse in a quiet stall and do not disturb him. An agitated horse with choke may inhale some of that saliva and end up with lung problems on top of everything else. Some chokes eventually move down into the stomach on their own, but most horses need help. Your vet will tranquilize the horse to relax him and will prob-- ably pass a stomach tube to help push the food along, using small amounts of water and keeping the head low so the horse doesn't in- hale anything. Very stubborn or large chokes may need surgery, but this is not common.

Founder feeding?

I have an 18-year-old mare that foundered last year due to obesity. I've been advised to not feed her any grain. Would you tell me more about taking care of foundered horses?

JR/Mt. Iron, MN

The best feeding approach is to start with one pound of high qual- ity hay per 100 pounds of body weight per day as your basic feed. This will maintain weight on most inactive horses.

One reason for not feeding foundered horses grain is that it is de- sirable to keep the horse's weight down, and grain is a concentrat- ed form of calories.

Another reason is that grains that escape digestion in the stom- ach and the small intestine travel through to the large intestine where they are essentially fermented by the organisms that live there. It is this process that changes coarse plant materials, like grasses, into something the horse can absorb and use for food.

However, in the case of more simple carbohydrates/grains, the fermentation produces acids that change the environment inside the intestine and may favor the growth of harmful bacteria. These harmful bacteria produce toxins that can be absorbed and result in founder.

It is possible (but not proven) that a horse that has foundered may be more sensitive to such toxins and later experience a flare-up of the problem.

On the other hand, gross underfeeding may cause large amounts of body fat to be mobilized to meet the horse's energy demands, and this also could cause founder.

If you're helping your horse lose weight by decreasing her feed, reduce the amount you feed her by no more than 1/5 pound per day every 30 days until she reaches the desired weight. Or, better yet, give the horse more exercise.

If the horse is being worked and cannot maintain her weight on hay only, gradually feed a little grain at a time, beginning with ½ pound twice a day, waiting two weeks before increasing her diet to ½ pound three times a day. If she still needs to gain weight in two weeks, add another ½ pound a day.

Gradual changes and feeding small amounts several times a day rather than large grain meals is the best way to go.

Can I start riding my mare?

I have a 10-year-old Arab mare who foaled for the first time a few months ago. Everything is going well. She is a good mother and not overly protective. They are out in a 10-acre pasture with one other horse. We also have a 100' x 100' paddock that leads from the barn to the pasture.

We noticed that our mare is looking a little pudgy and in need of exercise. Would it be appropriate at this time to start taking the mare for little rides in the paddock and around the pasture? Or should I wait until the filly is weaned?

DB/Internet

Light exercise can be beneficial, but remember that your horse's tack won't fit her the same after foaling as in her more svelte days. Be sure to provide adequate padding.

There is no problem at all with riding your mare a few months after she's foaled. The small paddock is a good place to start until mom and foal get used to the idea. Be ready for some spooking, jumpiness and inattention until riding becomes a part of their routine.

Some of the "pudginess" you are seeing could be from stretched muscles that have not resumed their pre-pregnancy tone. Exercise will help this, too. But, before assuming the mare is overweight, evaluate her topline, hindquarters and ribs to make sure it is not just a stretched belly giving this impression.

As the foal grows, demands for the mare's milk will increase tremendously, often to the point that the mare is actually not capable of eating enough to avoid losing weight. Therefore, a little extra fat at this early stage is not necessarily a bad thing. Exercise is fine, but don't cut back her feed — she will need it.

Bowed tendon advice, please

I am 15 years old and have had my 12-year-old Paint horse "Spirit" for four years now. I rode him one morning and he was fine. By evening, he was lame. I thought maybe he stepped on a sharp rock. By 9 p.m., he could barely walk. A week later, our vet told us he bowed a tendon. I've asked many friends and experts about it. No one can tell me very much. Can you please tell me about it?

AS/Foley, MN

"Bowed tendon" is a rather loosely applied term that can cover a wide range of tendon injuries. A true bowed tendon is a tendon that has been torn, usually in the middle. There is a good deal of swelling and heat, and in severe cases (complete or near complete rupture of the tendon), the ankle will be dropped lower than the one on the other side when the horse puts weight on the injured leg (if he even will put weight on the injured leg!). Swelling of the tendon sheath — the tissue around the tendon — or simple swelling of the tendon without an actual tear will often be just as swollen, hot and tender at first as a true bowed tendon.

Tendon injuries are usually caused by working the horse at speed when he is tired. This can result from either working an unfit horse too fast or working any horse too fast for too long. Horses who are not worked every day, then are taken out and run, can injure a tendon. Even regularly ridden horses can injure a tendon if they get too much hard/fast work too often. Pounding at slower speeds on very hard ground could also do it. Riding on steep hills for long distances may also injure tendons. Less commonly, a freak injury such as riding in extremely heavy mud, stepping in a hole or getting caught in a fence and overstretching a tendon trying to escape may be the cause. However, normal, healthy tendons usually do not get injured easily.

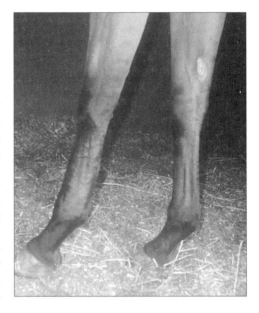

There are usually several instances of minor injury with minimal swelling, heat or lameness that occur prior to the day the horse actually hurts himself badly enough to be obviously lame. In some cases, the horse may have had an injury to the tendon in

This horse's bowed tendon (left leg) is past the acute stage, and the swelling is moderate. The horse is nearly sound, but could reinjure it easily.

the past that you never knew about, and this is what made him more likely to injure the tendon again.

There are lots of treatments offered for injured tendons, but the bottom line is that only time can heal the injury. If there is not really a tear in the tendon, healing may occur within a few weeks. More serious injuries take several months. Stall rest is advisable until the leg no longer feels hot and the swelling comes down. During that time, hosing, icing and wrapping the leg will help ease the inflammation.

Do not use "bute" (phenylbutazone) or other pain-killing or anti-inflammatory drugs, as these will only make the horse feel better than he really is and possibly make him put too much weight on the injured leg. Once the swelling, heat and pain are under control, the horse should be walked slowly for 15 to 20 minutes, once a day for a week or so, then twice a day. Cut the time if heat, swelling or pain return.

After that, turn him out in a large field, and let nature take its course to heal the leg. Make sure the horse is getting a high-quality diet with adequate levels of trace minerals (especially copper). Feeding a B vitamin and vitamin C supplement may also help ensure the tendon heals quickly and strong. All these nutrients are needed for proper healing.

Umbilical hernia normal

We are interested in purchasing a weanling filly to eventually use as a broodmare. We fell in love with her conformation, as well as her pedigree. One concern was pointed out to us by the current owner — she has a hernia. What are this filly's prospects as a broodmare. Is this a genetic flaw?

F & SU/Walton, WV

Umbilical hernias may be hereditary but are not necessarily so. It is impossible to tell without tracking down the members of her bloodline. Small (about the size of a quarter) umbilical hernias (like "outie" belly buttons) are fairly common and cause no problems, even in a broodmare. However, larger hernias are a significant weakness in the abdominal wall and could become larger and more complicated (i.e., bowel going into the hernia area) in advanced pregnancy. Your best bet is to have a veterinarian examine the filly and give you an opinion. If horse vets are rare in your area, a cattle veterinarian can also help — the problem is fairly common in cows, too.

Sole abscesses

My nine-year-old Quarter Horse gelding recently went lame and was found to have an abscess on his right front foot under the shoe. My veterinarian drained it and provided him with an Easy Boot, with instructions to soak his foot daily in Epsom salts and water for three or four days or until he was walking normally, and to then keep the Easy Boot on for three weeks, changing the dressing every few days.

The next day he was walking normally and even trotting in the pasture. The following evening he was again lame, this time in his left hind foot. I called my veterinarian again, he came out the following day, and guess what? Another abscess! However, my horse was no longer lame and therefore the abscess was not drained. Instead I was given a sole hardener to apply daily.

I would like some more information on what causes abscesses in the sole and how to prevent this from happening again. I purchased this horse last summer and had a pre-purchase exam performed with no mention of him having thin soles or a predisposition for foot problems.

My current veterinarian did mention that the front foot with the first abscess does have a thin sole. I do know that this horse had previously been kept in a stall at a boarding facility. I now keep him in a large pasture area. The pasture drains fairly well, and, although it obviously becomes somewhat muddy when it rains, it is not as boggy as some areas I have seen horses in.

Could being out in a pasture with occasionally muddy conditions cause this problem in a horse previously kept in a dry stall? If so, why did this occur now and not during the heavier rainy season months ago. What precautions or changes can I make to prevent this from occurring again?

AMS/San Jose, CA

Infections inside the hoof (which can be in locations other than right under the sole) can occur if there is a penetrating injury to the bottom of the foot (sole or frog), or infection can get in through breaks in the integrity of the white line. A horse with "flat" feet or thin soles (or soles that have been thinned too much by the farrier) is certainly more susceptible to severe bruising, which causes a collection of blood under the sole. This blood puddle is a great place for bacteria to grow. If

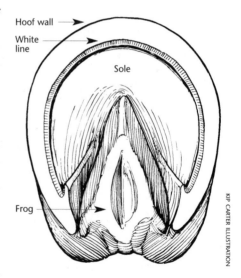

the bruising injury also broke through the sole, bacteria can get in it. However, this is not that easy to do, even with a thin sole — like trying to push a sewing needle through a finger nail.

Infection is more likely to get in if sole trimming is carried too far (you see pink tissue or even drops of blood) or through the white line. The white line can be accidentally punctured when applying shoes if the nail angle is not exactly right. The horse will "jump" when the nail is going in because he feels it. A more common problem, though, is small separations at the white line caused by the horse's toe being too long.

Bacterial numbers in a stall can actually be much higher than outside, and mud provides a good cushion for the feet. As long as the conditions are not constantly wet, don't blame your turnout. However, do check the field for any broken glass, half-buried wire, etc. — anything that could puncture the foot. It could also be that the horse has been carrying the abscesses around for a long time. It is not uncommon for a horse to have a foot abscess drain, but then turn up with another one in the same foot a year or more later. Draining abscess material from a foot is very difficult. It can move around and be located in many little pockets, not causing problems until the amount of material is great enough to cause pressure.

For prevention, ask your farrier to avoid taking off much sole. The more sole is left, the better protection. Pick the feet regularly to check for injuries along the frog, and have dead frog trimmed away. If your horse's toe is too long, begin to have it trimmed back. In the foot as God designed it, the white line is only about ⅛ of an inch wide, and the distance from the point of the frog to hoof wall no more than ⅓ of the distance from point of frog to back of foot.

Reading a feed bag

Can you explain the percentages given on feed bags? For example, my 50 lb. bag of alfalfa cubes says it has 13% protein. If I fed my horse 10 pounds of cubes a day, how much protein is he getting?
JP/Internet

The percentages listed for protein on a feed bag refer to what percent of the feed is protein. So, if you have a 10% protein feed, 10% of the weight of the material is protein. For practical purposes, you can assume each pound of feed had 1.6 ounces of protein (10% of 16 ounces). There is actually slightly less, since even hays and grains contain some moisture.

There are 2.08 ounces of protein in one pound of your 13% protein feed, (13% x 16 ounces). So feeding 10 pounds gives your horse 20.8 ounces, or about 1⅓ pounds of protein.

Feed bags may also list a percentage for fat and for fiber and/or ash. You can assume the remainder is carbohydrate, minerals and vitamins. (Carbohydrate content is not listed per se.) The major minerals — calcium, phosphorus, magnesium, sodium, chloride and potassium — are listed as grams/kg of feed or as percentages. Trace minerals such as copper, zinc and manganese are listed as ppm (parts per million) which is the same as mg/kg of feed.

Fresh-cut grass

I have a question about fresh-cut grass. I am sure I read somewhere that you should not feed grass cuttings to horses. Is this true? And if so, why? Also, I am getting ready to mow the field. Do I need to remove the horses from the cut grass there? Please help. I don't want to endanger my horses.

DW/Internet

Just about everybody has heard the taboo against feeding grass clippings, but nobody seems to know why you shouldn't. Common reasons NOT to feed clippings are:

1. Chemicals: Lawns that have been treated with fertilizers and herbicides may not be safe to feed. Better to be safe than sorry, if your lawn has been treated with anything other than lime.

2. Fermentation: Grass with a high moisture content will ferment quickly if left in deep piles. However, you can pick up the grass within an hour or so of mowing and feed it safely without worrying about fermentation.

3. Choke: Short lengths of clipped grass may not stimulate the horse to chew as well, and a ball of grass could become lodged in the esophagus on its way to the stomach, resulting in choke. This is theoretically possible, but how often it actually occurs is anyone's guess (choke is typically more of a concern when feeding older horses or horses with a history of throat problems, like soft-palate displacement). Choke actually is usually more of a potential problem with low-moisture feeds like hay, rather than grass, which has a high water content.

4. Founder: The horse is not any more likely to founder from grass clippings than he is from grass he "cuts" himself and eats. No special precautions are warranted on account of a fear of founder, which is unlikely.

We know of many horses who have been fed generous armfuls of cut-grass clippings without developing any problems. That's not to say nothing could ever happen, but if your horse is not prone to colic or founder from grass, is not being fed grass from chemically treated lawns, and has no history of choke, you can usually safely give him a few pounds of fresh clippings in a bucket or hand-feed it.

There are some special precautions about leaving horses in a pasture that has been mowed. Fermentation is more likely to occur when mowers are used that leave the clippings in high, deep rows. If growth was not dense at ground level (i.e., a field with a good percentage of clover or alfalfa), and the grass cut very short, the horse may be tempted or forced to sample the mounded-up grass clippings and could develop digestive problems. The mounded-up grass will also kill growth underneath, just like it does on a lawn. Mowers may also panic some horses and could cause them to injure themselves.

If at all possible, remove the horses from the field while it is being mowed. The best arrangement is to try to find a local farmer interested in baling the grass in exchange for all or part of the hay yield, and leave the horses off until it has been baled. If you can't do that, mow often and before the grass gets too thick and high. Leave grass long enough that horses will be willing to graze the remaining growth. Mow the field back and forth, and side to side, to break up any deep rows of cut grass and to expose the cuttings to as much air as possible for quick drying. Try to mow when the weather is predicted to be hot and dry for a few days; the lower the humidity, the better.

Tail chewing

I have a four-month-old colt who chews on other horses' tails. This colt was orphaned at birth, is getting the best of feed, and is out in a pasture all the time with one or two ponies, but chews their tails. I've tried putting cayenne pepper on their tails, and nothing seems to work. What can I do?

SE/Drewsville, NH

Tail chewing in this case may be partially behavioral and partially nutritional. An orphaned foal of this tender age is likely to still have a very strong "oral fixation." It is common to observe foals making mouth/chewing motions whenever they approach another horse.

Since the ponies cannot be nursed, the foal may have fixated on their tails. A repellent is the obvious answer, although you have tried some without success. We suggest you try RAP LAST (J.M. Saddler, Inc. 800-627-2807, 210-646-8488), a spray-on product designed for horses that chew their bandages. This product works well on the most determined chewers.

You could also try a full-length tail bag, which could double as a fly swatter for the pony. However, a determined foal would probably easily get this off.

It's not unusual for foals to occasionally chew on another's tail, but if it becomes a pattern, a nutrition deficiency is likely.

On the nutritional end, one theory is that tail chewing (like other forms of depraved appetite) is related to a trace-mineral deficiency. This is a good possibility since the minerals in mare's milk are believed to be highly absorbable and the most suitable to the foal's immature digestive tract.

You can improve trace-mineral digestion by adding active yeast cultures to the feed — assuming the foal will eat it (many horses are not crazy about the smell or taste).

Starting the foal on Ration Plus (800-728-4667, 804-438-5590), a liquid added to the grain or hay, will encourage the development of a strong, healthy population of micro-organisms, also encouraging better absorption of trace minerals.

One major problem is that most routine diets are deficient in trace minerals to begin with. Providing trace-mineral salt blocks will not solve the problem since these are formulated for dairy cows and do not provide adequate levels of some minerals. Plus, you cannot guarantee the foal will voluntarily take in the required daily amount.

The entire ration (hay and grain together) must be balanced to include all-important trace minerals as well as correct amounts of calcium and phosphorus for growth. Unless you feed a complete feed for growing foals, this is not likely to be the case.

If you are using a grain fortified for growing foals, a good product for you would be Opt-E-Horse (Weaver Leather 800-932-8371, 330-674-7548), which contains excellent levels of copper and zinc, the minerals most likely to be deficient in the hay portion of your horse's diet.

If you are feeding a "regular" horse diet, consider using a complete vitamin and mineral mix such as Milk & Grow from Uckele (800-248-0330, 517-486-4341).

As for the ponies, optimal regrowth of hair will only occur on a high-quality diet with adequate vitamins and minerals.

Wolf teeth explained

Could you clear something up? Do horses of both sexes have wolf teeth?
RW/Internet

Yes, horses of both sexes have wolf teeth. Many people confuse wolf teeth with canine teeth, which usually erupt only in males. Wolf teeth are the first premolar (first cheek tooth), while canines are

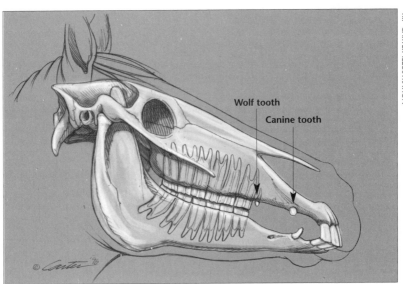

Wolf tooth

Canine tooth

KIP CARTER ILLUSTRATION

It's not uncommon for the bit to bump against a horse's sensitive, erupting wolf teeth, causing him pain. Young horses, especially, should have their mouths checked by a veterinarian if any bitting problems arise.

located closer to the front of the mouth, near the incisors.

Wolf teeth may or may not erupt completely. When they are located just under the gum line but don't come all the way through, they are called "blind" wolf teeth. The normal age for eruption is five to six months.

Wolf teeth sometimes cause problems with bitting, particularly if they are only partially erupted. In this case, having them extracted is often recommended.

Girth itch

I'm wondering what "girth itch" is. At the stable where my four-year-old gelding is in training, almost all of the 25 horses there have had it. Apparently it goes around through the flies and is passed to the horses. They used an antibiotic spray on him. Is there anything you can do for this, and how long does it take to get rid of it?

JP/Internet

The term "girth itch" can be used to describe just about any skin condition in the area of the girth/belly — from a simple equipment rub to an infection. In your case you are probably dealing with either a persistent fungal infection or a seasonal (warm weather) problem caused by larval forms of a parasite in the horse's skin, also called "sweet itch."

The fungus is spread by contact with infected equipment, such as girths, sponges and brushes. The larvae come from biting flies and are buried in the skin where they cause an angry, red, open reaction.

To treat a larval skin problem, the horse should be wormed with ivermectin. Some veterinarians recommend treating the horse with antihistamines or steroids before doing this to help prevent a serious allergic reaction when the ivermectin kills large numbers of larvae in the horse's system. Check with your vet.

For a barn-wide fungal problem, drastic measures will get quick results. Web or cloth girths or fleece girth covers must be washed in hot water and bleach or disposed of. Leather girths must be cleaned after each use. All sponges in use should be disposed of and replaced. Soak all brushes in a solution of 1/4 cup bleach per gallon of water and then dry them in the sun. Buckets used for bathing should be wiped out completely with full-strength bleach, rinsed well and dried in the sun. Antibiotic creams or sprays will not work too well on a fungal infection and could make it worse by killing off normal skin bacteria that would compete with the fungus. Use either an iodine-based shampoo or scrub with at least 0.7% iodine (check the label) or a chlorhexidine-based medicated shampoo with at least 4% chlorhexidine. You can get these through your vet or possibly at a farm-supply store in the dairy-cow section.

Subject: Sensitive skin

Can you please help? I have a friend who just purchased a nine-year-old Quarter-Thoroughbred gelding whose skin is very thin. The horse had not been ridden in about a year. After putting a saddle on and riding for only an hour, the skin was rubbed raw from the breast collar and girth. Is there anything he can do to toughen up the skin, or are there vitamins he should feed the horse?

J/Internet

Nutrition is important to skin, but if his skin looks healthy otherwise, he is just having an irritation problem. An hour is too long to ride a horse who is not used to being ridden. Make sure the equipment fits properly, perhaps even asking a professional to look at it. Pad everything with sheepskin or other soft material. Keep all equipment very clean — clean after each use, even the padding/covers.

Ride when it is cool so that excessive sweating does not complicate the problem. And groom the horse well before riding. If you increase the riding time gradually, starting at just 10 minutes, his skin should adjust well.

How cold is too cold?

My wife and I are keeping our horses at home for the first time and don't know when to keep the horses inside due to weather. We have a 10-year-old Quarter Horse and a six-year-old Paint, both mares. We live in western Pennsylvania. Both horses were boarded previous to this year, and the barn had the philosophy that "they are best off outside as much as possible," so they should be used to being out in extremes.

What is the rule of thumb for keeping the horses inside, as opposed to outside and blanketed or unblanketed out in pasture?

BB/Zelienople, PA

Unfortunately, this is one of those circumstances in which hard and fast rules don't help much. On one extreme, you would have to get

Winter clothing is appropriate in cold weather, especially for body-clipped horses.

to sub-zero temperatures and wind chills before worrying about such things as frostbite and hypothermia. However, if your concern is (as it should be) animal comfort, avoiding stress leading to excessive weight loss or increased susceptibility to illness, the answer is quite different. Horses, like people, tolerate cold much better than cold with wind, simply in terms of how content they are to be out in it. Even teen and single-digit temperatures are much easier to deal with if the sun is out, the horses are dry and the wind isn't blowing.

Individuals vary in their tolerance to cold depending on the amount of body fat, the density of their hair coat and how accustomed they are to being out in the weather. Blankets are optional for dense-coated, well fleshed-out horses. But thinner-coated, thinner skinned and skinnier horses or older horses definitely benefit from blanketing. If a shelter is available and positioned to block the prevailing winds, a wider range of conditions will be tolerable.

The ideal situation is free access to the barn/shed/stall from the pasture, letting the horses make up their own minds. If shelter is not available free-choice, leave them in when it is raining or snowing (the snow will melt when it hits the horse and soaks through the hair) and any time temperature or wind chill gets near zero.

Otherwise, take your cues from the horses themselves. If they are shivering, standing with their rears to the wind and not moving around or eating, standing at the gate all the time, bring them in. Don't forget the No. 1 health threat to horses turned out in cold weather — colic caused by inadequate water intake. Water the horses a minimum of twice daily, and use hot water (it will cool to drinkable quickly) to encourage them to drink. Many horses will not drink very cold water or will not drink enough water.

We agree that horses who are accustomed to the temperatures will stay much healthier than those who are not, but by all means keep those doors and windows open all winter unless precipitation or drafts are coming into the stalls.

How long to ride?

I have a 3½-year-old Quarter Horse gelding whose knees have just been confirmed as closed. He grew fast, so he is still immature looking, although my vet has said he is structurally ready for anything. I started him in early September. How long would you recommend I stay in the saddle? I've been up on him for 10-15 minutes for the first six rides, now I'm up to 20 minutes. We are just walking, giving to the bit, learning to modulate speed, stopping, moving the hip and so forth.

CH/Internet

It sounds like you're doing everything right. Gradually increasing the time in the saddle at the rate you are doing is fine. You are wise to question the time in the saddle, though; the bones of the spine are the last to "close," some still growing until the horse is around five years old.

It is difficult to give you an upper limit for riding time because that would change depending on what you are doing, how well-balanced you are in the saddle and how strong the horse's back is. It would be ideal to use two sessions instead of one long one. Be sure to watch for the following early signs of trouble:

1. Swelling or heat anywhere on the legs. Check front and back, all surfaces, not just joints, and remember to make it routine to feel the temperature of the hooves daily.

2. A change in the horse's attitude and behavior, such as ear pinning, tail swishing, swinging the hindquarters, shifting weight from foot to foot and/or changes in how he reacts to brushing or touching. These behaviors may all indicate early back pain.

3. Development of touchiness along the back, anywhere between the high point of the rump and the withers. Horses respond differently to touching and grooming their backs — some sink down on pressure, some tense up a little.

Is cribbing contagious?

I have a cribber, and some places won't take him for boarding because they say he'll be a bad influence on the other horses. I'm willing to pay for any repairs they might have to make to their barn if he chews on anything, but is cribbing really contagious?

LM/Internet

Cribbing is a behavior in which the horse grasps the ends of an object, such as a stall door or fence rail, and flexes his neck and throat muscles, like he was drinking through a straw. Cribbing is not the same as wood-chewing, when the horse gnaws on a fence, usually due to boredom. Cribbing is more than a bad habit. Studies have shown that cribbing actually has a soothing effect on a horse — his

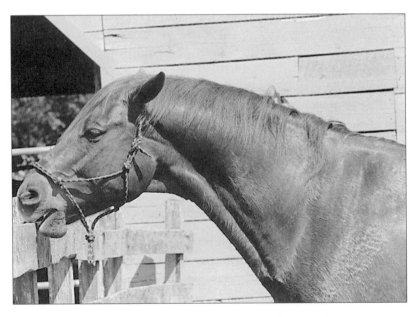

This experienced cribber will crib the moment his collar is removed. Note the flexion of his neck muscles and his total preoccupation with what he is doing.

heart rate actually slows while he cribs, and horses who crib have much higher levels of endorphin in their blood than noncribbers.

Many people don't want a cribber in their barn because they are afraid the other horses will pick up this bad habit. However, studies of barns/farms that have cribbers usually show that only a few (maybe even just one or two) of the horses crib, although other bad habits/vices may be evident in the other horses.

Some (although not all) foals of mares who crib do develop the habit. It may be more likely for the foal of a cribber to begin than for another adult horse in the vicinity, although we could not find good statistics to prove this. The foal is more likely to imitate his mom, perhaps because he has inherited the genetic and chemical make-up that makes this activity especially pleasurable.

So cribbing is not contagious, per se, and because a horse is stalled next to a cribber does not mean that the horse will begin cribbing. Some barns are stressful places, however, and when a horse lives without adequate turnout, regular exercise and grooming, pleasant surroundings, feeding times, etc., he's more likely to look for stress-relieving behaviors, such as wood-chewing.

Alternative to bute?

A year and a half ago, my 23-year-old Quarter Horse mare was diagnosed with articular ringbone in her right front pastern and with degenerative joint disease in both hocks (the right much more so than the left). Since then, I have been feeding her glucosamine. This has helped her hocks a little bit, but her ringbone has become rather severe. Despite these problems, she is still a happy, energetic, healthy horse.

Just recently, I read about feeding aloe plant extract or supplements to horses with injuries and chronic problems. Would feeding aloe supplement in addition to the glucosamine help my horse move about easier? If so, which supplement/extract do you recommend?

Also, I occasionally give her phenylbutazone if necessary to help relieve her pain, but I do not want to "bute" her every day. Is there a natural, holistic pain reliever that is safe to give every day?

CK/Buellton, CA

Advanced ringbone is one of the most difficult lamenesses to treat. You are dealing with a combination of joint/cartilage damage, which is a problem with any type of arthritis, and mechanical interference with movement and pain from a build-up of bone around the joint.

Effective arthritis supplements are aimed at helping the cartilage, but this is only part of the problem in ringbone, as you have found out! It is unlikely that changing supplements will give your horse much more relief. We suggest you continue with the glucosamine to combat any further joint cartilage damage with the ringbone or in the hocks.

In addition, you need adequate, safe pain control. Magnetic bell boots may help your horse. We have had some success using these in other ringbone cases. Choose your boot carefully, however. You need one that fits so that the magnets are positioned at and just above the coronary band. The magnetic material should be in the form of strips or cards (these are usually about the size of a credit card or slightly smaller). The smaller round magnets may work if there is a generous number of them and if the boot fits with them in the correct position.

Phenylbutazone may still need to be an important part of your management plan. Daily use is not advisable, but when you really need it, use it. Correct shoeing/trimming is also very, very important, and you will need a very skilled farrier to determine what approach is correct to take in this individual case. In general, the heel will be slightly lower but always keeping the angle of the foot and pastern normal (i.e., with the bones properly lined up). Squaring or rounding the toe and/or use of any shoe that is designed to permit easy breakover will usually help ease pain. Pads and other shock-absorbing materials may also help.

The aloe vera plant has been praised as having soothing and healing properties for a variety of conditions, but not all aloes have this benefit. *Aloe Vera Barbadensis Miller* is generally believed to be the most potent plant. We can't say for sure that aloe would help your horse (or that it wouldn't!). If you want to try it, you should get a liquid aloe preparation or an aloe gel and either mix with the feed or give by dose syringe. Use six times the recommended human dose.

Are magnets correct to use here?

About 14 months ago my 18-year-old mare foundered quite severely. The initial treatment provided by our original vet was, unfortunately, the wrong one, and her condition worsened. However, with great help from our farrier, we found a specialist — both in shoeing and veterinary care. With a lot of work, special shoeing and cutting her tendons, her coffin bone went back into place. That is the good news. The bad news is she has had chronic abscesses in her feet ever since. We now seem to have conquered the one on the right foot, but the left one continues and seems to be getting worse. We have used antibiotics — both in her system and packed in the abscess. We have soaked her feet in CleanTrax, in hydrogen peroxide and in merthiolate/DMSO.

In the last two weeks, I have been using magnets on her hoofs. I have two questions: Am I potentially harming her by using the magnets, and can you suggest any other approach for the abscesses?

TOB/Internet

As a general rule, magnets are not recommended in the presence of infection, but in this case things might be different. Magnets stimulate blood flow. Of course, for the blood to flow, normal blood vessels must be present. Clotted/blocked blood vessels are one of the consequences of founder and are why the attachments of the coffin bone to the hoof wall come loose in the first place. The magnets will stimulate blood flow through the remaining healthy vessels, which helps get oxygen and infection-fighting cells and antibodies to the area. The increased blood flow can also make symptoms of inflammation worse and might actually increase spread of infection in otherwise normal areas; but in this case my guess is they would help her foot get back to a more normal level of blood supply.

You will need to carefully monitor her feet every day. If the magnets are working, her hooves will feel warmer when the magnets are in place. However, if the pastern sweats under the magnets, the foot feels too hot or the lameness worsens, stop immediately and treat with cold water soaks until her feet have returned to normal temperature.

Pulsating electromagnetic therapy (this requires coils and a battery to generate the current to produce the energy fields) on low settings and frequencies below 10 can actually fight infection.

As for alternatives, it sounds like the only other avenue that might be open to you would be to have a portion of the sole or hoof wall (depending on location of the abscess) removed so that the infection can be directly drained, exposed to air and treated. After all that you have been through, I am sure this is not an attractive option, but if the alternative is for the infection to settle in her coffin bone (difficult, if not impossible to treat) and destroy all your hard work to date, it might be something to consider.

Another option to explore with your vet is the choice of antibiotics. You might have a "bug" that is resistant to common antibiotics or that requires a course of intravenous antibiotic treatment to get things rolling. **PH**

24

Dear John:
Readers Share
Tips and Stories

We often hear that experience is the best teacher and that we can learn from other people's experiences, as well as our own. So we are sharing the best reader tips and stories from *John Lyons' Perfect Horse* Magazine.

Sentinel: Still on duty

I purchased a 21-year-old Thoroughbred for $1 last year. His owners planned to put him to sleep because he had gone blind. This ex-intermediate-level dressage competitor now has a new lease on life and a "second career," thanks to you, John.

I learned about your methods in 1995 after acquiring my first horse — a "rogue" Appaloosa. I wanted a relationship with him like you have with Zip, so I set out to learn all I could. I attended one of your three-day clinics but, because I couldn't trailer my horse that far, I was horseless. I sat in the arena praying for a horse to ride — and you announced that Sentinel, a blind horse, was being given away.

I realized immediately I was meant to have him. You allowed me to ride him in the clinic and I learned that, with the right training, a blind horse can do most things a seeing horse can do.

I now ride Sentinel for pleasure and in the sheriff's mounted patrol. This past year, he led our Christmas parade and worked parking-lot duty for a George Strait concert. He has been relatively easy

Sentinel is dressed for a Christmas parade. Twenty-one years old and blind, he's enjoying his "second career."

to train and doesn't spook at much — after all, he can't see "scary monsters."

Working off a cue system, I have taught him to lift his legs, almost as if marching, enabling him to go up a curb, over a hill or step up into a horse trailer. Teaching him to give to the bit has allowed me to ride him almost anywhere, safely. He seems aware of trees and fences, and doesn't run into them when turned out in the pasture. Except for occasional nicks to the skin and a few bumps, he maneuvers around his stall adequately. He even turns to face me when kissed to and comes directly to me. (Sometimes my seeing horse won't even do that!)

He does have a tendency to pace in small circles (we like to tell people he's self-lungeing). But, other than that, he's a joy. I would encourage others to consider ownership of a blind horse, although not without caution.

LB/Kingsville, TX

Round pen for committees?

I read your editorial, "Our Actions Tell the Truth," (see page 41) just in time. Simply cross out the word "horse" and substitute any of the following: child, spouse, co-worker, neighbor, friend... I'm sure you get the picture. As editor of my church newsletter, I was struggling to get out my last issue. None of the committees had submitted their information (let alone on time). Everyone was just as crabby and stressed as I was. My computer was messed up, my husband was traveling, and the kids were sick. The editorial I had written as a send-off was a pretty caustic whopper. To top it all off, I had no time for riding, so my attitude was really poor.

Well, I got to your paragraph about Jesus setting a good example. Hey, none of us are perfect. So, I rewrote my editorial in a more humorous vein, stopped yelling at the kids, got a good night's sleep and spoke nicely to my church members when I called them on the phone. Decided to "let my actions speak louder than my words." Your advice works both on horses and people and made my week easier. Now, can you write an article on round-pen work for committees?

CW/Boxboro, MA

Parallels in life

Your magazine and videos have made a world of difference in our family. Four months ago, my son was diagnosed as autistic. I was devastated, but I knew God would be with us through this.

Last September a friend lent me an entire year of your magazine, and I read every one with fervor. At the same time we were having my son evaluated because of some behavioral and developmental concerns. As the weeks and appointments went on, the problem was becoming more apparent, although I remained in a state of denial. In the meanwhile, I stuck to those magazines, keeping my focus on something other than my son.

When the final diagnosis came, things got worse before they got better. Beginning school for him was difficult, and I had to be my son's advocate and most important teacher. So, I gritted my teeth and started reading. I immersed myself in books on autism and stories of autistic people overcoming their handicap. To help give me a diversion, I watched your videotapes. I knew I had to hold on to the horses to get me though the quagmire of this unknown "thing" that had kept my son a stranger for so long.

As it turned out, the methods used to work with autistic children paralleled your "conditioned response method" with horses. I was so excited! The whole time I was leaning on your method for strength and sanity, I was being given all the tools I needed to reach my son.

Now, months later, my son has language (he recently started calling me Mommy!) and plays games with the family and wants to be a part of our world. It all started with one basic principle — define the goal, then break it down into the smallest possible components. Now, when I want to accomplish something with my son, I look for a starting point and develop a lesson plan, as you've taught. The results have been incredible.

WS/Jefferson, NY

Reprogramming works

I have a yearling Arab who injured his hind fetlock, so I had to change dressings on that leg. I wanted to do this with him loose in the middle of the corral, but I found myself trying to keep up with his moving foot. This made me mad, so I jerked on his head, then I tried squeezing him in a tight place, then I tried spanking him. Pretty soon he was kicking out when I touched his foot. All of a sudden I saw myself all hot, sweaty and mad, and my horse scared and defiant. Not only was this not safe, but it was absurd. I had to laugh. I flashed back to having heard you talk about how equipment does not control the horse. Well, I had certainly proved that point!

I took a minute to regroup. Then I tried the same theory you use when working with a cinchy horse. I would reach for his leg, but stop just before he moved his foot. In a half hour, he held his foot still while I rebandaged it. Thank God, horses (and, especially, humans) are reprogrammable!

BH/Okanogan, WA

First spray in two years

Some horse people I know wouldn't even admit to owning ponies, but I'm not one of them. I have a three-year-old Welsh cross pony that we believe was abused before I bought him as a yearling.

He tends to be skittish about some things, and genuinely freaks at spray bottles — until recently. I tried your technique of rubbing the bottle all over him and then gradually worked up to spraying while I rubbed the bottle on him. No fits! I was able to spray him with fly repellent for the first time in two years.

LO/Plainview, MN

Relinquishing authority

The other day it dawned on me what "giving to the bit" is about. The horse I was riding is a Morgan and has a head-set from his show days — it looks good, but he has no idea what "giving to the bit" is.

He locks up when he's ridden into the ring. Just walking away from the gate he's ready to rear, spin and go out the gate.

Slowly and patiently I asked, and he started giving to the bit. Eventually I made it around the ring (without him balking and wanting out of the gate), then we started jog, canter, leg yields and so forth.

His owners are happy with his turnaround, yet I still know I have a long way to go with him. On trail rides with other horses he reverts and ignores my requests, wanting to charge ahead so he can lead. I know we have to work on giving to the bit in the company of other horses and when he's excited, but we're making progress.

Most folks are so indoctrinated about a horse having a head set that they never really see the softness and relinquishing of authority that a horse can give us when he gives to the bit. This horse helped me to see that the other day. He looks awesome, but when he's in that head-set position, he's the boss. We have a way to go yet to get that light, soft response all the time.

RA/Torrance, CA

Learning cycles hit home

Why didn't anyone teach me this before? Knowing about the learning cycles a horse goes through, being aware that a horse often responds out of fear or emotions, finding out the importance of taking baby steps, of breaking down the training into clear and simple tasks and the value of repetition has done wonders for me.

When Willow Run was being trained to load (properly), just the knowledge of the cycle — that she wouldn't do it, then would do it, then wouldn't again, before she finally got it — saved both of us a lot of frustration.

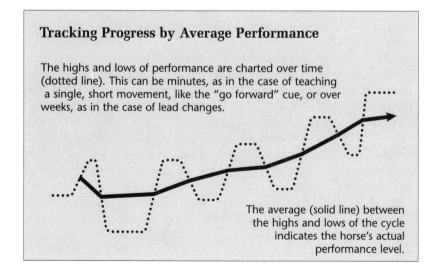

Tracking Progress by Average Performance

The highs and lows of performance are charted over time (dotted line). This can be minutes, as in the case of teaching a single, short movement, like the "go forward" cue, or over weeks, as in the case of lead changes.

The average (solid line) between the highs and lows of the cycle indicates the horse's actual performance level.

Ever wonder why your horse loads one day but not the next? He may not have gone through all the ups and downs of the learning cycles.

In the past when we would get to the "bad again" stage, I'd change what I was doing, thinking that what I had been doing must be wrong. I was usually tired by this time, and my response, I'm embarrassed to say, would be real frustration. Phrases such as "What's the matter with you?" will never again come out of my mouth. Now I stay true to clear cues, and pretty soon she's doing it great.

Recently we ran into a problem jumping. Although I'm a dressage rider, my mare had always done just fine when we jumped little jumps. That was until the day someone came out to look at her to purchase for their child. She wouldn't even go near the jump. I thought, "How would John analyze this?"

So I started to break it down. It seemed she was emotional about trotting to the jump, so we started walking to it. She would approach it just fine at the walk but was still excited about walking over it, so I broke it down even further.

All we did was walk to the jump. When she would go all the way up to it calmly, we started walking over it again, but this time she wasn't emotional. We did this 75 times!

But my old ways started creeping back. Next we tried trotting the jump — NOPE, this was too large a step; we had to break it down further. When she would trot close to the jump and walk over calmly, I knew we could again try trotting the jump and guess what? Success! *Perfect Horse* is a "Five Nicker" publication!

By the way, Willow Run is now doing wonderfully. She is living with a new owner — a little girl who adores her, and a subscription to *Perfect Horse* was thrown in the package by me.

JAH/Columbia, TN

Voice of experience

As a veterinarian, I have had to deal with a few poorly handled and very aggressive stallions in my time. It isn't a pretty sight, but when they are re-schooled, they become very mannerly and manageable. I love what John says about it. People have to realize that biting horses must be taught their limits with no uncertainty about who is in charge; otherwise, they are likely to try to push those limits even further the next time. Timid owners should not have stallions.

My experience has been that some horses, particularly stallions, will test every new person who comes to work around them. The horse may be well behaved around the owner, but will try to intimidate a new handler. New people should be warned about this and instructed how to handle the challenge, or they might get hurt or overreact and hurt the horse.

It is common for a horse to charge or make a mock charge when the new person enters the stall. I have found it helpful to teach the horse to go to the far corner of the stall and stand, facing the person. Have the person tell the horse "Get back!" and point to the desired spot. These directions can usually be used by anyone who can manage a commanding tone of voice. From then on, they can proceed as with any horse. It pays to teach a cue that you and others can use with your stallions or other "chargy" horses.

DEK, New Hope, PA

"Don't shy" cue for riders

You're right. There is no "don't shy" cue just for horses — but there is one for their riders. As novice riders who came to horse ownership as adults, my husband, Tim, and I were determined not to be trapped on our property by the fear our horses might shy on the trail.

Tim's hard-luck mare, who had been bullied into spookiness by abusive former owners, and my arena-raised baby, who saw crocodiles behind every bush, were a challenging pair. Add to that, two adult riders acutely aware of the brittleness of bones. It could have been an impossible situation.

However, Tim and I worked on developing our riding skills, especially balance, and we learned to focus our horses' attention on us. On the trail we would point out things that could be problems — not to prompt our horses to spook, but to guide them around potential hazards. This taught us to be observant of our surroundings and our horses' reactions. When something potentially scary came along, like a plastic bag caught on a bush, it became second nature to calmly move them past the offending object.

Using a philosophy of "I see it. It's not a problem," and "Relax and move on," we've put in hours on the trail without a lot of "horsey hysteria." Those few times when something did provoke some side-stepping and white eyeballs, we could stay relaxed in the saddle and move with the horses calmly.

JH/Reno, NV

Perfect relationship

Some time back, I had just gotten my mustang, Job, and it was basic round pen work for both of us. As Job was going to the left, he had his head high and facing to the outside of the fence. As he traveled around I thought about the kind of relationship that I wanted to establish with him. I would have really appreciated an "I'm here" relationship. Of course, I can imagine he was thinking of a "turn me loose" relationship.

I took the thought of relationship one step further in wondering about my relationship with Christ. I wondered how many times I have gone around the round pen, as it were, keeping my head high and refusing to acknowledge that Christ was at the center. It's taken me at least 30 years to get focused on Him. I sure hope it does not take me that long with Job.

Christ didn't give up on me, and as long as God will bless me with Job, I won't give up on him, either. As the Bible says: "Being confident of this, that He who began a good work in you will carry it on to completion until the day of Christ Jesus."

LK/Internet

Smooch worked

I decided that it was never too early to start teaching cues to my weanling. I began working on "smoochie" noises so that he would turn and face me and eventually come when called. Because he's so young I don't tax his attention span but just play with him at it. So far, the cue works about half of the time, but just enough to avert a potential disaster.

I was grooming him in his stall, and one of the barn dogs got in. During my attempt to chase the pooch out of the stall, the baby got out and headed down the barn aisle toward where the roofers had just been working and had left nails on the ground. I kept calling and walking after the colt to try to catch him, but he wasn't slowing down.

I finally thought to try "smooching" to him. When I did, he stopped dead in his tracks, turned his head and walked to me. I reached for his halter and quietly lead him back to his stall.

I thank you for what you are teaching everyone who loves horses, and I'm sending you a "smoochie" from the two of us.

SD/West Orange, NJ

Winter mittens

One reader reports that wearing a winter mitten helped her teach her horse to give to the bit. Instead of letting the reins slip through her fingers, as she usually would have, she made a fist with her mittened hand and braced it against the saddle. In no time the horse figured out he wasn't going to move her hand, so he "gave" to her!

Thanks for the great suggestion, NW!

Rebuilding confidence

You are right when you say that we should trust our instincts. I have been riding my whole life. I grew up in Maryland where my family raised Thoroughbreds for the track. After my first two horses, both of whom were a bit crafty but safe, I found myself gentling and eventually breaking our young horses. All of the horses we raised were quite sociable and had good temperaments. It was a fine experience, and I gained an easy rapport with horses in general.

As a teenager I thought that nothing could stop me. I was able to ride throughout college as my parents were kind enough to let me keep my horse near school. After college, I was determined to reach for the brass ring — I signed on as a working student for a big dressage/eventing trainer. It did not prove to be a good match.

The second bad step happened a few years later when in graduate school. I began riding with a man who was a strict disciplinarian, and when he said "jump," every horse and student did. I rode with him for six years. I have no idea why I stayed so long, some type of brainwashing effect, I think.

After several years as his student, I bought a five-year-old, 17-hand ex-racehorse from him. Although all appeared fine for a while, it became increasingly obvious that whips, spurs, martingales and tight reins were having a bad effect on this basically timid horse. Fortunately, I never rode him in a strong bit. Even though I was listening and trying to follow this trainer, my old instincts started whispering to me that things were going downhill fast.

My horse had always been pushy, but he started biting, shoving and, worse, not only shying, but bucking, bolting and eventually rearing under saddle. It was the rearing that eventually crushed my confidence and sprained my back twice. The advice I was getting for the rearing — to hit him and/or drive him forward — was not working. My horse was terrified and had reached the end of his rope.

Then I read about your "giving to the bit" exercises. I started ask-

ing my horse to give to the bit a little, and this gave me my first tool in what has become a long struggle of rehabilitation for me and my horse. Because it became difficult to remain on this trainer's farm when I wasn't taking lessons and was beginning to have a bit of success on my own, I finally left. That was a year and a half ago.

Due to his owner's diligence, Magic is now a well-behaved horse. But, it required going back to basic horse-handling exercises.

On my own for the first time in many years, I started listening to my instincts again. We started over with a new farm, new techniques and new tack — Western. I started collecting every article of yours that I could find, and we've worked slowly, waiting until we have one lesson down before we go on to the next.

Although he will probably always test authority, Magic's ground manners are now excellent, the best of any horse that I have owned. He stands ground tied, comes when I kiss to him, no longer bites or runs off when I turn him loose. He is respectful of my space, leads and pivots without a halter (in enclosed spaces) and watches me whenever I'm near him. And, most amazing, he seems happy and eager to get out and do things. I can actually watch him think a problem through.

We are now working on "giving to the bit" and turning right and left (can you believe a second-level dressage horse not knowing how to turn?), all of this at the walk and in a safe arena so far. It makes me sad that I'm no longer the confident rider I was several years ago, but I hope that in time, my courage will return.

My husband has asked me why I don't just sell this horse and buy a quieter one. But, I can't. First of all, I want to get over my fear of this horse, not some quiet pony. And also, I don't want anyone to get hurt or to have shatter this horse's trust again. I know he can be a perfect horse, and I'm going to keep working at it until he is.

SLW/Tucson, AZ

Trailer success

I would like to relay a trailer-loading episode that happened at a trail ride I was attending. I was waiting for my ride home and was watching a women trying to load her horse. She used every method she could think of, but the horse refused to load. After she accepted for about an hour and a half, I offered to give her a hand.

I didn't have my dressage whip with me, only a shorter riding crop, so a friend tapped high on the horse's hip while I stayed to the front of the horse and "supervised" the nose and front feet. I told him to stop tapping the moment there was any forward movement. Using this method, we had the horse on board in about 15 minutes, we had the horse on board. I mentioned to the owner that the horse needed more work at home to make sure he understood the lesson, and she was extremely grateful and promised to follow up with it. My friends were amazed. It was great to be able to be of help.

SB/Alden, NY

A cue to paw

I'm 38 and never had horses when I was younger, so I had some pretty dreamy notions about them loving me and me riding off into the sunset. HAH! But I've had horses now for three years and, fortunately, I found your method early on.

The greatest thing happened when I had to teach my two-year-old Morgan gelding to load in the trailer. I set aside time, as you suggested, to teach him the "go forward" cue. I worked one hour the first night and quit when the horse put both front feet into the trailer.

At one point I thought I had taught him to paw the trailer floor. I'd tap and he'd paw. Then I'd stop tapping, as I considered this forward movement. It continued: I tapped he pawed, and so forth. Eventually he started leaving his feet in the trailer.

We were at it again early the next morning. In two hours he was loading and unloading like a pro.

I was so excited. I'd raise my whip above his hip, and he'd step in. I was speechless. I put him away because I was afraid I'd bore him with the exercise.

My husband came out 15 minutes later, so I ran to get the horse so I could show him our new accomplishment. He was pleasantly surprised, but not as excited as I was (but then he wasn't the one who had just stood tapping for two hours!).

Now we can go anywhere. And I did it myself!

CB/Baldwin, WI

Crossed the bridge

After a lifetime of wishing for a horse, Excalibur came to me four months ago. He's 32 and I'm 53, which makes us a perfect match. I've seriously read, watched and studied all I could about horse care, tack, training and riding. Your *Perfect Horse* and symposium tapes have inspired me to treat Ex no differently than I would any other horse — safely, calmly and consistently.

Last week we crossed a bridge and a milestone in our relationship. He was afraid to cross the bridge. We approached; he stopped. Instead of making a big deal about it, we looked at it, turned back and rode closer to it the next time. On the fourth approach, he marched across that one-lane wooden bridge like a confident, frisky guy. And we learned how to handle it from you. Thanks.

JP/Anchorage, AK

Check him out first

I recently purchased a green-broke mare that I was assured had been professionally trained and had lots of foundation ground work. Oh, how I wish now I had taken the time to work her through the basics myself before getting in the saddle.

Instead, I swung confidently aboard and immediately realized my mistake. She tensed, her hindquarters dropping from beneath me, then in a moment of trembling, she exploded upward. I'll spare you the rodeo details, but she fell to the side, somehow missed crushing me and jumped back up before I could get off. She stood there trembling for minutes. Neither she nor I wanted to breathe for fear we would set the whole thing off again. Eventually she relaxed and walked off a few steps. Then I was able to get off.

At a later day, I took her to the round pen, teaching her to respond to specific cues and to trust me. She and I are buddies now, spending hours at a time roaming the hills. Thanks, John, for having taught me that there are no bad horses, just untrained ones.

I learned my lesson. Miraculously, neither of us was injured. Never again will I take a horse at face value or anyone's word about a horse — I'll check him out myself.

TP/Grants Pass, OR

Thanks for your story. I don't get on a horse unless I have seen someone else ride him first. I treat him as an unbroke horse until proven otherwise. Keeping to that rule has saved me from a lot of potential wrecks.

Lesson plans matter

My reason for writing is to say that goals and lesson plans are really important, and I want to encourage others to take your advice and write out a plan for their horse.

I got my first horse when I was 50 — a yearling Arab-Quarter Horse — not a good choice for a novice. She has always been too feisty for me, and although I planned to sell her several times, I never did because I loved her and thought she'd be a good horse someday. Now, several years later I also have a second horse.

I listened to you teach about the "calm down" cue at Equine Affaire and decided when I got home I'd teach that cue, but I thought my horses were pretty well trained otherwise.

I started lungeing them before going on to teach them to drop their head ("calm down" cue). As lungeing didn't go well, I decided to go back to square one in the round pen. Imagine my surprise when my Arab started kicking, bucking, fish-tailing and just plain ignoring me. This happened two days in a row.

My goal — well-trained horses — had been too narrow. I ended up writing down what I thought a well-trained horse meant — standing tied, leading, being brushed, trailering, coming when I call, lowering the head on request, and listening to rein cues. I graded both horses on each item, which helped me to determine what each horse needed to work on. Then I listed my special goals for each one — like parade riding.

When you follow a lesson plan, your time is not just being wasted because you don't know what to do next, or what you want to accomplish with your horse.

PM/Beulah, MI

Trailer conversion recommendation

My husband and I have become interested in camping and trail riding at a distance from our home, so we've been shopping for a horse

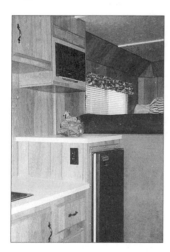

trailer with living quarters. The prices of trailers are shocking enough, but the addition of living quarters can almost double the cost. My husband called some RV dealers, who supplied us with names of people who would convert dressing rooms into living quarters at affordable prices. By doing that we can buy our own appliances and have the area built to our specifications.

One thing to note: We found that if you are planning to finance the trailer through a bank, they may require that the person or business doing the trailer conversion have special credentials, such as being RVI approved.

We hope this can save somebody some money, or give them an idea about how to go about fixing up a trailer they already own.

The dressing room/tack area of a new or used horse trailer can be converted to a custom living area as the one above.

MS/Foxboro, GA

Riding where we can

I attended Equine Affaire and was among the bleacher people you let sit along the ring. It was a wonderful experience. What was the most helpful was the idea that there is a lot you can do with your horse without ever getting on his back. That took a lot of pressure off me and gave me permission to step back and work on training my gelding without the rush (from myself and others) to ride him. That, and the WESN lesson (a real breakthrough for us), made an incredible difference. My gelding now knows what to expect, and he trusts me. We are now "riding where we can, not where we can't" and loving every minute of it.

SB/Cleveland, OH

No longer feeling guilty

I just had to write to tell you how much I appreciated your comments about the importance of just having fun with our horses. It really hit a nerve with me.

I lost my first horse due to a positive Coggins test that just came out of nowhere. He never showed any signs of illness, and, in fact, at the time I was conditioning him for an out-of-state trail ride, which was the reason for the Coggins. Fortunately, a friend had an isolated cattle ranch where my horse could live and satisfy the quarantine laws. He lived many happy retirement years there, but I never got to ride or even see him again. It helped a lot that our last ride had been long and very enjoyable for us both.

I have had my second horse, a beautiful and multi-talented Morgan, for 14 years now. Because of DJ's looks and abilities, I have been under considerable pressure to "do something" with him — show him, jump him or get competitive with the dressage that I like to play with — something. I have often felt guilty when I opted to just go for a trail ride instead of schooling. This, despite the fact that DJ is a truly wonderful trail horse and loves the trail every bit as much as I do.

We will continue to work on our dressage-y stuff, but I will never again feel guilty about just going out and doing what we both love. He is 18 years old now, and while he is in perfect health, as you say, we never know how much time we have.

Thanks also for helping me solve the few little problems he and I have in spite of our extremely close relationship. DJ is a very sensitive and alert horse and can get a little wired sometimes. I now have a signal that he can really understand for me to communicate to him that it's ok and he can relax. He really appreciates it. I am getting great results using what I learn from you.

SM/Warsaw, IN

Cowboy is teaching Frisky to give to the bit. He takes all the slack out of the rein until Frisky gives, as he's doing in this photo. Then Cowboy releases the rein — at his owner's command.

Anyone can do it

I thought your readers would enjoy some pictures. This is our dog, Cowboy, on Frisky, a young horse my husband just started working with under saddle. As you can see, anyone can do it!

After the last picture, Cowboy fell off the horse, remembering to release the reins. Cowboy is wearing clothes, as our young daughter does not believe anyone should be "naked" in public.

Cowboy helps us in our training (although usually not from in the saddle) and is better trained than the kids. By the way, our kids complain we treat them like animals. In our minds, that's not such a bad deal!

MB/Los Alamos, NM

Creative solution worked

Currently I am training a five-year-old mare. She had a neck injury at the age of two, and all training was stopped. Her injury healed completely, but the breeder had 70 colts that year and she was forgotten.

For the last three years she has been on 1,000 acres of pasture. She was upset, scared and nervous when her new owners brought her to me for training. I gave her a couple of days to adjust to her new surroundings and started by getting her to come to me in the paddock. She was not even used to being touched.

As scared as she was, she never showed any signs of aggression. She did a great job in the round pen the first three days. I praised and loved all over her.

Well, on the fourth day she was going right, she reversed to the left on cue perfectly and went about six feet and tried to reverse back right. I prevented her from turning back, and she stopped with her rump to me. I smooched and bumped her with my rope on her left hindquarter. She flinched and began shaking, but she would not move an inch. I stepped back and smooched to her, and she turned and faced me perfectly like the day before.

I started her to the left, and she went about four feet and tried to reverse. I bumped her on her right (outside) shoulder, and she turned back to the left but froze again. I threw the rope at her hind end, and she just stood there shaking, worse than before.

I have been riding horses for 33 years and training for the last 25. I did everything I knew. I walked up to her and calmed her some, stepped back and tried to get her to take one step forward. She was frozen in place.

She was getting more and more upset all the time. I stepped to the middle of the pen, toward her front end, and smooched to her. She turned and faced me. I continued smooching and she came to me, but she was still shaking.

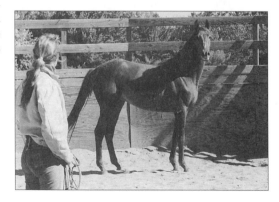

It's important to know when to revert back in the lesson to an easier step.

I have never had this happen before. I have always been able to get them to move forward to the left and right. After thinking about it a few minutes, I decided to put on her halter and lunge line.

I started her walking a small circle around me. She began to calm down. Gradually I let the lunge line out, increasing the size of the circle. She went around twice to the left, and I stopped her, rewarded her and quit for the day.

The next day I lunged her in the round pen right and left. She did it perfectly with no hesitation or fear. I took the halter and lunge line off and began working free again. She went around once to the left and tried to reverse. I stopped her from reversing, and she stopped rump toward me.

I bumped her on the right shoulder with the rope, and she turned left and stopped. I bumped her in the rear and smooched. She went halfway around and stopped, but she did not try to reverse. Yeah!

In no time she was going left smoothly. I have never used the halter and lunge line to solve a problem in the round pen. But, then, I never had a horse do this before. Even a lazy horse will move after being popped with the rope in the hindquarter. My question is: What would you have done?

LC/Haskell, OK

You did exactly the right thing. When you reached an impasse, you backed up in the lesson and found a simpler way to explain to the horse what you wanted her to do. The way you know you did the right thing is that your horse did what you wanted, no one got hurt, and your horse was calmer at the end of the lesson than at the beginning.

The rule is: Go to a place in the lesson plan where you can ask the horse to do something and have him do it 100 percent of the time. Build on that control. Also, as you found out, almost anything you can do in the round pen, you can do with a halter and rope, if the horse is halter broken. We only use the round pen to have a safe way to begin a horse's training.

Start the kids out right

I just wanted to let you know how much I enjoy your teaching. I always wanted to be a horse trainer but realized it wasn't the horses who had a problem. So I decided that the kindest thing I could do for the horses was to start teaching kids (since most adults already know everything).

I'm not a certified instructor, but I use your system with all of my students, ages six and up. Since it is step by step, most of them grasp it easily. (We often don't give kids enough credit.) OK, giving to the bit can be monotonous, but they hang in there and in doing so have made major changes in their horses. Most of the kids don't have enough money to go and buy a "made" horse. But we have had great success reschooling problem horses and bringing along young ones.

Each horse has a wonderful story, like Gypsy who used to pull back and couldn't be bridled, who now can be tied safely and bridled by a little child, to Leroy, a confirmed puller who had to be ridden in an elevator bit. He is now in a full cheek snaffle and soft as can be. Little things, but big differences. I love it when my 10-year-olds try out a horse for sale and tell me where the horse isn't giving through the body and on which rein he is resistant. Pretty good for kids.

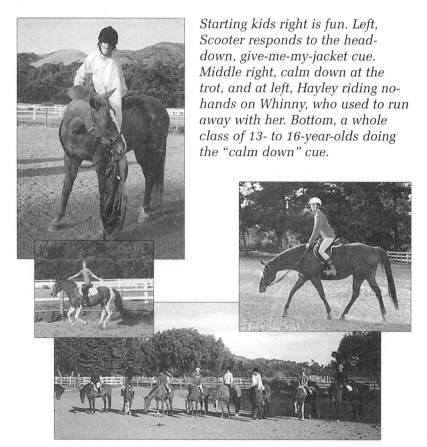

Starting kids right is fun. Left, Scooter responds to the head-down, give-me-my-jacket cue. Middle right, calm down at the trot, and at left, Hayley riding no-hands on Whinny, who used to run away with her. Bottom, a whole class of 13- to 16-year-olds doing the "calm down" cue.

Training kids right from the beginning with your methods will not only make a lot of happy horses, but I think will give the kids great communication skills, respect, compassion and patience. That's what makes this a rewarding job for me, and you have made it that much easier.

SM/Carmel Valley, CA

They played it safe

My friends and I enjoyed Equine Affaire and put our new knowledge to use the next weekend.

We had planned to take a special trail ride — a 20-minute walk would take us to the county park with miles of marked and manicured trails. It was to be our last ride together because I was moving my horse to a new barn. We'd all been together except Sandy, who was nervous that her horse would have to cross a creek. I assured her we'd only have to cross a small stream on our way to the park.

Unfortunately, the small stream had gotten a lot wider since last fall and the now fast-moving water created a little gully on one side. We were proud of Sandy's horse for negotiating a small overflow a few yards away and hoping she would follow us across. Our fearless leader was a big Thoroughbred with a long, confident stride who would walk through anything — as long as he was first.

Next came a little gray Arab who didn't like water but was so well trained that he marched slowly through on a loose rein.

When it was my horse's turn, he plodded through without paying much attention to the water. He was busy looking at the sheep in the next pasture (he hates sheep).

Sandy asked her horse to go forward, and she did to a point, then stopped. Sandy admitted fear (she's intelligent). We told her, "Hey, that's a Lyons' rule — if you're afraid, don't do it!" Another rider, Lori, who has a calming way with horses, offered to ride Sandy's horse across, and the rider switch was made.

With gentle persuasion, the mare moved a few inches closer.

Lori asked, "How long does John Lyons say this will take?"

We replied, "Maybe three hours." Sandy only had two hours as she had a plane to catch.

We decided to try the buddy system. So I came back across the stream, then started across again, hoping Sandy's horse would follow. It didn't work.

We ended up saying, "This is too hard for her. We'll have to take her back to an easier place and let her practice." (See, we are trainable.) This was better, and Lori had her crossing a muddy trickle several times, but now she was moving close to the high-tensile wire surrounding the sheep field. "If she backs a foot through that wire, she'll really get hurt." "Hey, that's a Lyons' rule, too — the horse can't get hurt." Sandy decided to take the mare home.

We all joined her. Our special last ride together had not gone as planned, but I consider it successful in a lot of ways: Sandy didn't get hurt, Lori didn't get hurt and the horse didn't get hurt. Sandy made her plane, and I didn't have to deal with any sheep.

SD/Bridgeville, PA

Horse faces down bulldozer

I was given this horse by a friend who was fed up with him. He bit, bucked at shows and spooked at his shadow on trail. More than once she had to walk him home from a trail ride. He reacted violently to brush around his legs (what fun!), didn't want anything to do with moving water and wouldn't load into a trailer.

After riding in one of your clinics in '94, and armed with your tapes, I was ready to make a change in this horse's life. I worked with him for about nine months

Looking at this horse with an umbrella and who-knows-what attached to him, you would never think he was given away because he was too spooky.

on the trail and another six months with a round pen and canyon trails to straighten out his other problems.

After two years he was turning, stopping, backing and rating his speed. He became so calm on the trail that our then 11-year-old daughter complained he was sleepwalking. He even drank from streams.

One day, when a friend was riding him, we had to go past a bulldozer. I looked back to be sure she was coming, and I caught my breath. That little trooper was frightened, but stood still and faced the dozer as it went by. My friend knew the horse before I owned him and was amazed at how well he controlled himself. She could tell how scared he was. I was proud of him and glad I spent time working with him. He is a changed horse.

JW/Anaheim Hills, CA

Leading, not leaving

You saved the day. Larry is an ex-game horse I'm trying to turn into a trail horse. Larry is the worst trail horse I've ever owned, but I love him dearly and over the past three years, we have come a long way. Sometimes he actually drops his head and walks. Isn't that wonderful!

Last Saturday, as my friend and I ambled (well, she ambled, we pranced along behind her) through the woods, we came upon a fallen tree. My friend and her young Arab stepped calmly over the tree. Larry, of course, said "Oh no, I don't think so." When he gets like this, he's very stubborn, and if you keep pushing, he rears (not a good thing!)

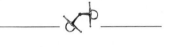

LYONISM ...

IT'S MY JOB TO FIGURE OUT WHAT CUE THE HORSE ISN'T RESPONDING TO, THEN TEACH HIM THAT CUE

So, I tried for a lower part of the tree, which he also refused. After several minutes of urging, squeezing, kicking and cajoling, I got angry, got off and attempted to drag him across the tree. (He was stronger than me.)

He would actually walk up and stop at the same spot each time. I got angry, called him a few names (that didn't work either), and wasn't any further than I was to begin with.

My friend recently started subscribing to your magazine, and she calmly told me what she read in one of your articles. This was easy for her, since she was on the other side of the tree.

"OK, OK," I ask, "what would John do?" Holding the bridle with my left hand, I started tapping him high on his buttocks. "You're irritating him," she said (I like this man already, I thought).

After 10 or so minutes, Larry started kicking. "Oh yes," my friend said, "he's supposed to do that." After five or so more minutes, he was backing away. What's wrong with this picture?

"Yes," said my friend, "he's supposed to do that, too!" By now my arm is falling off, and my face is red from anger. I get back on the horse, deciding it would be easier to irritate him on his back. Ten more minutes of tapping, kicking, backing, he takes one step forward. I stop. We do this for another five minutes or so, and he just walks over that tree.

I was exhausted, but we did it. John, I think your methods work. I was ready to tie Larry to a tree (preferably the fallen one he would not step over) and leave him.

DM/Moravia, NY

Take care when retraining

A lot of people — from my vet to my chiropractor — ask me the same question: "Why do you put yourself out rescuing these abused horses?" My answer is always the same, "Because someone mistreated them, and they deserve the chance to prove what they can truly be."

Many people in our area get a couple of acres, then fulfill their dream of owning a horse. We've all heard of the person who gets a "baby," so they can learn with them — AAUGH! What I have dealt with are the disasters that come from those who sought no help. Their neglected horses were the result, i.e., worms, starvation, overgrown hooves and no training.

SK purchased this four-year-old stallion from people who starved him to keep him docile. Humane Society action prompted them to sell him. It took hours of work to be able to touch his face after his ingrown halter was removed and he healed. He has ended up a good-looking and well-mannered horse.

Just as bad, they'll hire a "trainer" who teaches them that chains, whips, even frozen garden hoses are necessary to train horses.

I'm not sure how many horses over the years I've re-started and trained, but I know for a fact that a majority would have been sold for meat had I not. Instead, they are loving, loyal and trustworthy companions. The only hope for the unfortunate horses are people who are willing to teach them to trust and how to behave. I am thankful for your magazine, tapes and book which I have shared with many.

SK/Tacoma, WA

Good for you! I'm sure most owners of neglected horses never intend to neglect or abuse their horse — ignorance or bad advice usually is at fault, as you mentioned.

I just want to remind anyone planning to work with a neglected horse of the three rules of training — that the trainer (you) should not get hurt, the horse shouldn't get hurt, and the horse should be calmer at the end of the lesson than at the beginning. Horses that have a lot of fear can be dangerous. Don't let your sympathy for the horse's condition override sensible horsemanship.

Blind team-roping horse

I have a blind companion, who happens to be an Appaloosa. His problem is due to severe cataracts. He is 20 years old and has been with me for five years. He was blind when I bought him from a man who was going to send him to the killers. I rode him for five minutes and bought him on the spot. How long he had been blind no one knows, because he had been laid up for two years after

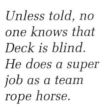

Unless told, no one knows that Deck is blind. He does a super job as a team rope horse.

bowing tendons in both front legs. The owner bought him because he knew his reputation as a roping horse. He didn't realize about the blindness until "Deck" ran into the wall at feeding time.

I still team rope off him and have done numerous other activities such as team penning, barrel racing and fun-days riding. The first time we went penning I rode with a man who was sitting third in the state standings, and the only thing he could say was, "Get yourself a team." He didn't know the horse was blind. Nobody does until I tell them, then you see their mouths drop open. They say, "He must really trust you." I like to think he does.

Deck is to be credited with saving the life of another blind horse. My shoer had a client whose favorite horse went blind. He told the client about Deck, and the horse was saved from going to the killers.

Not all horses have the mentality to cope with the situation, but with Zip's plight known on a nationwide scale and Deck's on a local basis, it shows people that there is hope, and reason not to give up on our companions.

CB/Arcadia, CA

Joke's not on her anymore

We want to tell you about a transformation. Our spoiled, spooky, Arabian alpha-mare-with-an-attitude, who I bought three years ago (and threatened to sell many times over), is now heavily into what I call the "Good for you" stage, due to my using Lyons techniques in her training. Also, I have learned to appreciate her sense of humor — now that the joke's not on me!

We also want to tell you about our "John Lyons baby." Our Thoroughbred broodmare gave us a fabulous, but feisty and inquisitive, foal in 1998, sired by a Connemara. He's always looking for trouble, which means that we have had to administer first aid to him often. Your gentle but firm approach has made all the difference in our care for him.

His last caper resulted in a four-inch head wound (lots of bleeding) and a neck wound. We were able to put pressure on his head wound for the 10 minutes required to stop the bleeding. This was critical because, due to the nature of the injuries, we were not able to put a halter on the horse. "Traditional" horse people had let us know that they thought training a foal was quite unnecessary, but it has paid big dividends for us in everyday handling as well as in these medical emergencies.

CO & DO, Canada

Basic rules for horses

One reader found this being passed around on email.

The art of snorting: Humans like to be snorted on. It is your duty, as the family horse, to accommodate them.

Neighing: Because you are a horse, you are expected to neigh. So neigh — a lot. Your owners will be happy to hear you protecting the barn and communicating with other horses — especially late at night. There is no more secure feeling for a human than to keep waking up in the middle of the night and hearing you, "Neigh, neigh, neigh..."

Chewing: Make a contribution to the architectural industry ... chew on your stall wall, the fence or any other wooden item.

Fresh bedding: It is perfectly permissible to urinate in the middle of your freshly bedded stall to let your humans know how much you appreciate their hard work.

Dining etiquette: Always pull your hay out of the hay rack, especially after your stall has been cleaned, so you can mix it with your fresh bedding. This challenges your human the next time they clean your stall — and we all know humans love a challenge (that's what they said when they bought you as a two-year-old, right?).

Doors: Any door, even partially open, is always an invitation for you and your human to exercise. Bolt out of the door and trot around, just out of reach of your human, who will frantically run after you. The longer it goes on, the more fun it is for all involved.

Nuzzling: Always take a *big* drink from your water trough immediately before nuzzling your human. Humans prefer clean muzzles. Be ready to rub your head on the area of your human that you just nuzzled to dry it off, too.

Holes: Rather than pawing and digging a *big* hole in the middle of the paddock or stall and upsetting your human, dig a lot of smaller holes all over so they won't notice. If you arrange a little pile of dirt on one side of each hole, maybe they'll think it's gophers. There are never enough holes in the ground. Strive daily to do your part to help correct this problem.

Playing: If you lose your footing while frolicking in the paddock, use one of the other horses to absorb your fall so you don't injure yourself. Then the other horse will get a visit from the mean ol' vet.

Shots: Humans are characteristically nervous when providing veterinary care for you. In order to soothe them, raise your head immediately after an injection. Humans seem to be comforted by swinging back and forth on the lead rope while screaming primeval noises.

Shoeing: Humans are creatures driven by instant gratification. After shoeing, trot smartly around to show your human how nice the shoes fit. The next day, drag one foot when you walk, to provide your little busybody with yet another project to work on.

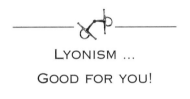

LYONISM ...

GOOD FOR YOU!

Visitors: Determine which guest is afraid of horses. Rock back and forth on the crossties, neighing loudly and pawing playfully at this person. If the human backs away and starts crying, swoosh your tail, stamp your feet and nicker gently to show your concern.

Children: Human children require much nurturing in order to develop a healthy self-ego. Never offer your right-lead canter to an adult rider. However, permit the child the honor of the right lead. Older children may be denied the first one or two canter cues, in order to prepare them for adulthood. Very young children *must* be given the right lead on the very first try.

Marriage: Your personal human attendant may also have a spouse, who professes nonequinity. Whenever your attendant brings the non-equus spouse to visit, you are to lavish unimaginable amounts of charm on the non-equus spouse, and more importantly, you must act fearful of your personal human attendant.

Ballet slippers: Your human attendant will often risk his safety by wearing shoes that might not provide full protection from hazardous ranch situations. You can correct (not punish) this behavior by applying pressure to the unprotected foot. Humans are known to move away from pressure, but only after making loud noises. Keep pressure applied until your human responds correctly to this cue.

Perfect horse wanted

LN thought our readers would enjoy singing this song she found on the internet. Imagine yourself sounding like Janis Joplin:

> Oh Lord, won't you buy me
> > A horse that won't buck?
> I'm tired of trying
> > To land standing up.
> I spend all my time
> > Brushing dirt off my butt.
> Oh Lord, won't you buy me
> > A horse that won't buck?
>
> Oh Lord, won't you buy me
> > A horse that won't bite?
> I count all my fingers
> > And toes every night.
> I feel like a carrot
> > When I'm in his sight.
> Oh Lord, won't you buy me
> > A horse that won't bite?
>
> Oh Lord, won't you buy me
> > A horse that stays clean?
> I brush him, I groom him,
> > I've considered chlorine.
> His color's too chestnut
> > For a horse with gray genes.
> Oh Lord, won't you buy me
> > A horse that stays clean?
>
> Oh Lord, won't you buy me
> > A horse with some guts?
> This spooking and shying
> > is driving me nuts.
> And while you are at it
> > Make me less of a klutz.
> Oh Lord, won't you buy me
> > a horse with some guts? **PH**

25

But, I'm Scared

*Fear is a natural part of life — both for us
and for our horses. So, does that mean
it's something to live with or to conquer?
When a rider gets scared, what should he do?*

Fear is real, and no matter how much anyone wants to ignore or deny it, fear plays a major role in the lives of many horsepeople. In this chapter, we're going to blow some holes in the traditional thinking about being scared around horses, and then we'll suggest some approaches that should enrich the life of anyone who's had a wreck or is really scared.

Fear is good. It's healthy. It's our mind's way of telling our body that danger is present. God designed us with an early warning system that would put our body "on alert" when the situation warranted it.

But being "on alert" isn't comfortable. Our heart beats faster, our breathing gets shallow, and our hormone system throws us into a "fight or flight" pattern. We're glad the system works — especially if we were to be confronted by a lion, tiger or bear. But when we're confronted with something of lesser magnitude, we may get irritated with ourselves for what seems like an overreaction. Then we have to deal with conflicting emotions and emotional responses that seem beyond our control.

And "out of control" causes more fear. When we fear being out of control, thoughts of what might happen next can paralyze our rational thinking. Then, there's often pressure from other people or fear of failure, so the fear cycle continues. How do we regain control? Well, rather than "overcoming" our fear, we can learn to manage it, putting us back in the driver's seat.

Don't "cowboy up"

When a rider falls, everyone and his brother seem to take it upon themselves to help the fallen rider, often advising what they've heard others say, rather than what the rider actually needs. A fallen or frightened rider doesn't need to "cowboy up," to swallow his fear and get right back into the situation that scared him. In fact, getting right back on the horse he's just fallen off may be the worst thing a rider can do.

It's normal — and healthy — for a rider to feel some fear after a bad experience. Fear is common sense in disguise, a God-given warning system. Our body is telling us that we are not safe. And, in many cases, our body knows more than our brain. Let's look at what happens when someone has a bad experience.

Don't be ashamed to ask for help if you feel timid, and don't take any unnecessary risks.

Let's assume that a moderately experienced rider is on a horse who spooks, wheels around and bolts for the barn. Even if that rider didn't fall off, he may end up scared, particularly when riding that horse again or when back out on that trail. Unless something changes, that rider should be afraid of riding that horse in that situation. It's dangerous.

But let's say his well-meaning friends encourage him to go back out to the scene of the crime, on the same horse, the same day. Both horse and rider have experienced a rush of adrenaline, as well as the letdown that comes after that adrenaline rush. Their nerves are less stable, so to speak, than on the first ride, and they are probably both more tired. Added fatigue means thinking isn't as sharp, and physical responses aren't as good. The likelihood of living through the second ride may be good, but it probably won't be a positive experience. Just living through something won't help the person be less afraid, but having positive experiences will.

Regaining control

What if, instead of heading back on the trail, the rider returns to the barn and heads into a small corral or round pen to cool down the horse. While they are unwinding, the rider works on gaining control of the horse's hindquarters, thinking through what happened on the trail and deciding what steps he needs to take to make sure the situation doesn't re-occur. He asks himself what cue he wishes the horse had responded to instead of bolting away. Then he sets out to practice those cues.

Every day that week, the rider practices the control-the-hip lesson until he can stop the horse from a gallop. The following week, he works on "spook in place" lessons, teaching the horse to turn to face something scary rather than bolting away. And the rider also works on a better sitting position and getting more physically fit, so that he feels more secure in the saddle. One last lesson, the "calm down" cue, so that the rider can tell the horse in no uncertain words to calm down when he gets excited. Finally, the rider is ready to venture back out on the trail.

Chances are, even though it may have been a few weeks since the scary incident, the rider will likely be far less afraid, because the reason for his fear — the lack of control — has been dealt with. A success story.

On the other hand, suppose the rider isn't the go-get-'em type, and comes back to the barn shaken. Or perhaps the rider only can ride on the weekends. He can't risk another incident on the trail. What should he do? Here's where the rule "Ride where you can, not where you can't" comes into play.

The rider should ask himself what he can do with the horse and feel 100 percent safe. That may be just walking and trotting in the arena. No problem. That's the place to start. The rider should only walk and trot in the arena until he's so bored, or so confident, that he just naturally feels ready to make a more adventuresome move. The next step may be either a change of location — say, to riding in an empty pasture — or it may involve more speed in the same location. Whatever the choice, the rider should concentrate on gaining better control of the horse within boundaries where he feels absolutely safe, only changing one parameter at a time.

Fear is helpful

More people get hurt each year with horses than with any other animal. Nearly every time I work with a large audience, I ask people to stand if they have, or if they know someone who has, been seriously hurt working with a horse. About 90 percent stand up. It doesn't take brains to get hurt working with a horse, and many of us have done it. Instead, it takes brains to work around these horses without getting hurt, and fear plays an important part.

I tell people I don't want them to overcome their fear. I don't want to work around people who are not afraid of horses. Their lack of fear will not only get them hurt, but it may also get their horses hurt, and possibly me, too.

Fear actually keeps us safe because what may be OK for one person to do really isn't for someone else. And no amount of coaxing should push us to do what we don't feel safe doing. My son, Josh, does things that I wouldn't do because it would scare me to do them. That doesn't make me a coward — it may mean that I know my limitations. The things that limit me don't necessarily limit or scare Josh, and that's OK.

We should not put ourselves, or allow anyone else to put us, in horse-related situations where we feel afraid. We shouldn't do things that scare us. It doesn't matter what other people can do. I don't need to fight my fear, and you shouldn't, either.

Pushing down the fear and putting on a strong exterior may well get you hurt. If you don't feel safe up on a particular horse at a spot on the trail, get off. There's always an alternative. If you don't feel safe leading an excited horse, let someone else do it. I've learned that I don't have to make choices that put me in danger. I don't have to work through my fear.

You know the first two rules of horse training: You can't get hurt, and the horse can't get hurt. If you override your fear, you are likely to get yourself, your horse or someone else hurt, and nothing is worth that.

When you are scared, though, sometimes the hardest thing is to stand up to people who may have been riding horses lots longer than you have and who may try to tell you to stop being scared and "just do it." But they are not responsible for your safety — you are. I never turn over the responsibility for my or my horse's safety to other people, and I don't have to prove anything to myself or anyone else.

No matter how little you know about horses, you probably know more than you think you do. Everybody has an innate ability to know the right thing. Some days you may get the feeling that you shouldn't tie your horse to the trailer, or that you shouldn't go riding on a certain afternoon. Ninety percent of the time, that little voice is right. Don't let folks dismiss you as silly.

Fear of failure

Unlike fear of injury or fear of being out of control, fear of failure is worth taking a serious look at. Bulldozing over your fear irrationally can lead to taking unnecessary risks, and being immobilized by fear reduces a person's quality of life. Have you ever noticed that people who fear failure are frequently trying to live up to someone else's standard? One way of overcoming fear of failing is to determine your own yardstick. Set goals that are realistic, and put lots of little steps in your program, just as we do with the horses. The more steps in the plan, the more sure of success you'll be, and your confidence will grow as you meet each goal.

Ride where you can, not where you can't. Control problems frequently occur when riding in an open field with other horses.

If you don't practice riding at speed, you'll never be able to stop the horse when he's going fast. The more specific you are in your riding, the more control you will have.

So how do you deal with setbacks? First, realize they are inevitable but also that they are only steps to get to the next level. The important thing is to keep enjoyment in your learning and keep pleasure in your riding. Work for improvement, not perfection.

Remember that it's the journey to get the performance — not the performance in itself — that is really important. I can get on a horse and teach him to do a flying lead change in a relatively short time, but those lead changes aren't as meaningful to me as the ones I do on Zip. Bright Zip and I worked on leads and changes a long time, and now when we do a series of changes, I'm really proud of him. I remember all the things that we went through for years to get to the performance we now have. It was the times that didn't work well that I had to figure out what else to try, and that's what really advanced my training. Those setbacks or frustrations didn't represent failure to me, but learning opportunities. You can never fail as long as you continue to try.

What about failure in competition? It's tough, and there's only one winner per class. But if you work for improvement, develop a good plan and stick to it, eventually the trophies will come along. But it's also important how you win the ribbon. Some ribbons are worth more than others, not because of the size of the class but because of the effort it took to win them.

Just a note: Sometimes people don't realize they are scared but think they are just angry with the horse. They try to punish the horse, or yell at other people, in an attempt to deal with their emotions. Blaming someone else or the horse won't improve performance, so avoid letting fear express itself as anger.

Getting past fear

So what should you do if you recognize that your fear is a warning that you may be in danger, but you don't want to stay afraid? Determine a performance goal and write yourself a lesson plan to improve your control, just as the competitive rider develops a plan to improve performance. You can't set out to be less scared, but you can set out to develop better control of your horse's hips or to make better transitions from the canter to the trot, for instance.

But we know that a goal and a starting point are not the same thing. Your starting point may not have anything to do with riding. If riding scares you, then don't ride for now. Perhaps begin by grooming the horse or working on ground-control exercises. Remember that "the horse you lead is the horse you ride." A horse whose leading manners aren't good won't be very mannerly when ridden either. The more specific you can become in leading your horse, the better will be his response and your confidence, too. He doesn't care if you are on the ground or in the saddle when you use the rein, so teaching control exercises from the ground will enhance your control when you do start riding again. For instance, if your horse has a tendency to rear, teach him to drop his head on cue. Or if he's pushy on the ground, he's likely to not be respectful of your rein cues, either, so work on those.

Do you have to ride?

Remember why you have horses in the first place. Nothing says that you have to ride, or that you have to ride on the trail or ride a particular horse. It may be that you ride in your mind but you best enjoy puttering around the barn. Be honest about what level of activity you'll enjoy, then set out to do it. Whistling in the dark is fine for those little mildly anxious moments, but real fear — like that feeling you get when you realize you've nodded off at the wheel — is a powerful emotion and shouldn't be brushed aside or made fun of. Listen to your fear, then learn from it and act on it. **PH**

Notes

26

To The Rescue

When Barb and Marla faced off with a frightened filly
during the Washington state flooding in 1996,
their John Lyons training experiences
saved the day — and the horse.

It was, quite literally, a dark and stormy night when two Washington horsewomen braved rising flood waters to save a lone, scared filly from near-certain death by drowning.

Faced with having to rescue a pastured yearling who'd never been handled, Barbara Fredenburg and Marla Foreman did the only thing they could think of: They dug into their years-deep mental store of John Lyons methodology and stripped the techniques down to bare essentials.

Setting the scene

Usually, warm Chinook winds blowing across the Northwest bring a welcome respite from the region's cold winter weather. But during one week in February 1996, they brought nothing but trouble to the little town of Richland, Wa. As the Chinooks sent temperatures high enough to melt the mountain snows, the resulting runoff gorged the Yakima River, which overflowed its banks and flooded the surrounding countryside.

Along with its threats to human life and property, the floods spelled danger for all animals — including the many horses stabled in the area. Members of the local riding club formed a cooperative network to relocate as many horses as possible. By Friday of that week, Barb and her friend Marla had hauled nearly three

The next morning, the road was entirely flooded. The barns were under three and a half feet of water, and the water was still rising.

dozen horses to higher ground. Barb finally returned home sometime after 7 p.m. that Friday. The phone rang with yet another request. There was a young filly in a big pasture, and flood waters were headed her way. One problem: The filly was about 18 months old and had never been handled, much less haltered or trailered. The property owners had been trying in vain for hours to catch her and move her to safety. Barb and Marla were on the way.

As Barb and Marla arrived on the scene, the road was already being blocked off to traffic. It was dark and cold, and the flood waters were due any moment. When the women entered the pasture, they learned the filly wasn't alone. Besides the 20 or so people gathered to watch and help, there was an older mare. Several other horses had already been moved; the mare had been left as a companion for the filly who, everyone agreed, would probably become more panicky if left alone.

The pasture itself was too large to easily corner the filly or work as a good round pen. Still, the people had managed to herd the frightened horse into one three-sided area formed by an L-shaped line of fence and a barn wall. At Barb and Marla's request, they agreed to calmly, quietly and steadfastly become a human wall on the open end. The filly was now inside — and the older mare outside — of one of the most makeshift round pens of all time.

To make matters more difficult, a floodlight had been set up to provide much-needed lighting. It worked great when the women's backs were turned to it, but totally blinded them when they faced it.

By the book

To start, Barb and Marla decided to simply walk up to the filly and see if, by chance, they could catch her. She ran right through them and the barrier of people. "That's when Marla and I agreed, 'We need to go straight to John's techniques,'" says Barb.

Marla stepped in for the first shift, while Barb moved back to stand between her and the human wall, as an extra aid in keeping the filly within the pen. All along they were talking and thinking, "What steps can we skip to do this before the water comes?'"

For instance, since Marla couldn't easily and confidently turn the filly back against the wall of people, she concentrated on keeping the horse on the other end of the "pen." And, to avoid the floodlight glare, she stopped the filly only when the light was at her back.

Soon, Marla had the filly moving to the left and doing inside turns. "We decided right away that we didn't need the filly to turn both ways," notes Barb. "We just needed her to turn and face us, to stand still, and to let us get a halter on her."

Things seemed to be going well, but Barb noticed that the filly was kind of gritting her teeth in a sort of snarl. "It was an aggressive thing, and Marla's back was turned to it." Wanting to stop that action before it got out of hand — and wanting to give Marla some respite — Barb traded places with her friend and continued to work with the filly on moving forward and turning to the inside.

"One time, I caught her snarling at me and I told her, 'Stop that!'" Barb says. "That's when we realized we had to be firm with her. We had been holding back just a little from the method, trying to be extra careful because the fencing and the surroundings were unsafe. But after that, if she put her rump toward us, we swatted it with the halter and lead rope, as long as she wasn't on the people-side of our make-shift pen."

Getting one part

As the women became firmer with their requests to the filly, results got better. Still, time was running out, and they'd come nowhere near haltering the youngster. That's when they remembered a basic Lyons' teaching. "John says if you can get control of one part of the horse, you can get the whole horse," explains Barb. "I figured the only thing I could get was the filly's eye. I could get her to look at me."

John arranged a special award ceremony for Barb to congratulate her for a job well done.

That wasn't as easy as it sounds. "There were tremendous distractions, as dogs and people were herding sheep and other animals off the property," says Barb. "I had to concentrate. I was demanding, insisting that the filly only look at me and not at the distractions. I think that actually helped her to lock onto me and follow me sooner."

The only way Barb could get the filly's attention was with a halter and a lead rope. "I'd slap them against my leg to make some noise." she says. But the tactic worked. Before long, the filly was not just looking at Barb, but turning to face her and then following her. "But I still couldn't get that last two steps in to touch her," Barb relates. "Hundreds of times I walked toward her and then away. But, as soon as I'd raise my hand, she'd run."

Finally, Barb managed to get the horse stopping in a corner. "There, I could finally work myself in and stand just a couple feet from her," she says. "I was able to move with her — if she took a step to the left, so did I; if she took a step to the right, so did I. I was able to keep her between my open arms."

Finally, a touch

When the filly simply refused to let anyone approach her head, Barb moved in toward her shoulder — and made her first contact. "I reached out and scratched her withers, then walked away. She was fine. I did that many times."

Barb also realized that she didn't have to sack the filly out all over. "All we have to get is her head," she thought to herself. With one hand, Barb rubbed the horse's back; with the other hand, she began slowly working her way up the neck.

"She'd touch the horse, then back off," says Marla, "until she could rub the filly pretty good all over her neck, shoulders, and rear end — but still not her head."

Eventually, though, Barb was able to get her hand over and under the horse's neck and, finally, between her ears. When the filly remained relaxed under Barb's hand, the woman repeated the entire process with the halter and lead rope, rubbing them gently all over the filly. When the filly was tolerating this level of touch, Barb took the halter in her hands, then softly and quietly buckled it around the filly's neck only, letting the rest of the halter and the lead rope hang loosely in her hands.

Four on the floor

With a halter and lead securely attached to the filly, Barb and Marla could see the light of hope shining bright. But they still had to get this baby into a horse trailer — out in the open, beyond the pasture's perimeter. Time for another switch.

Barb handed the filly over to Marla, who'd brought a long, soft cotton lead rope from her truck. Barb then haltered the older mare and led her from the pasture to the horse trailer. Marla continued to work with the filly, "Touching, handling and teaching her to come forward with a tap on the rump — so we had at least a little control over her," she says.

With the mare loaded, Barb came back for the filly. Now in the open with no restraints beyond the halter, she remained manageable. In fact, says Barb, "When we got her to the trailer, she moved forward and put her front feet on the trailer right away. We let her stand there and then we backed her out once."

That's all they had time for. When they asked her to go forward again, they also asked her to put all four feet on the trailer floor. She did, and the ladies closed up the trailer and headed their rig toward drier realms. The next morning, the filly's pasture was five feet under water.

Lessons learned

Much later, Barb attended a John Lyons clinic where she accepted an award for her and Marla's heroic work. As John told the story to his audience, he brought up aspects Barb hadn't even thought about at the time. Most importantly, he pointed out how the women's initial patience and persistence had paid off in the long run.

For example, says Barb, "Since I had gotten the filly to follow me both directions even before I was able to touch her, we never had to pull on the rope when the halter and lead were on. We just asked her to watch and follow as she had done when loose. She was actually taught to lead before she accepted being touched or haltered."

The rescuee and her two rescuers a few months later.

And, Barb continues, "All the original work with the filly took a long time (1½ hours), but because we stuck with it, loading her into the trailer only took 10 minutes."

That also helped when Marla went to unload the filly, which she did without difficulty. "I handled her a lot before turning her loose," recalls Marla. "And even when we took her halter off, she didn't run away."

"Furthermore," adds Barb, "I understand that when the owners went to bring the filly home again after the flooding, they had no problems catching or trailering her."

Today, the filly is back in her pasture and perfectly gentle. "Her owners have had a saddle on her, and they've led kids around on her," says Barb. "She just continues to grow in confidence." "Yet," she adds, "without John's techniques, someone probably would have had to rope the filly or put her through a frightening experience. For me, this incident confirmed the power of John's methods." **PH**

Section III

Putting Theory
into Practice

27

Lyons On Lyons

Editor's note: So many readers want to know about John's personal history and background. We sat down and talked for a few minutes.

Perfect Horse: *Tell us about your younger years. Did you grow up in a horsey family?*

John Lyons: No. As a kid I was involved in a lot of sports, and I played three sports in high school: baseball, basketball and football, but mostly baseball. I was offered a chance to sign with the Dodgers as a senior in high school. But it wasn't enough money to keep me from going to college. In college I ended up playing basketball and baseball, and played baseball for the University of Arizona in Tucson. I actu-

ally didn't get into horses in a serious way until I was 23 or 24. But I've been involved with them ever since.

PH: *What did you do after college, and how did you get into horses?*

JL: I married Susie in my senior year. After college, I went to work on my stepfather's 3,000-acre farm growing cotton, sorghum and oranges. I then took a job with another company and moved to Dallas, then up to Cincinnati, Ohio, where I managed a manufacturing plant. After that we moved with a company that made surgical implants to Kansas City. In Kansas City, I bought some acreage and horses.

I built a really nice barn for the horses. One day I was cleaning stalls and decided I liked working with horses and cleaning stalls better than working in the medical profession. Less than a year later we bought a ranch in Colorado.

That was in '76 or '77. We had 350 cows — a cow-calf operation. We also collected a lot of horses, as horse people often tend to do, and we started showing them. When the cattle market went bad, we basically went broke. I started training horses full-time and doing clinics, back in 1980. I was also still showing horses. In fact, Zip was high-point champion in two regional clubs. In 1981 we hauled him to 11 shows, and he was high-point performance horse in 10 of the 11 shows.

PH: *Why did you start doing symposiums nationally?*

JL: It took seven years doing the clinics full-time before I could pretty much do as many clinics as I wanted to in a year and they would fill. A turning point came when I was doing a clinic in Las Vegas, and it was snowing. About 100 people were observing the clinic, sitting on metal bleachers for six to seven hours trying to figure out what was going on in the arena. I had a little tiny speaker system, and the people couldn't hear what I was saying. I felt there had to be a better program so people could be comfortable and see and hear well. That's when I designed the symposium format, geared for the observer.

We started looking at definitions of different words. We thought about the word seminar, which would be a normal word to use. A seminar is a group of people getting together to listen to speakers talk about a particular topic. A symposium is when a group of people get together to eat and drink and share ideas. We knew what we had in mind was a symposium.

PH: *Where did you learn what you know about horse training? Did you ever work with a big-name trainer?*

JL: I've never had the chance to study with a well-known trainer. There are two ways I have picked up what I have learned.

The first is in the clinics themselves. When I started doing the clinics, I accepted any horse with any problem. I guaranteed that I would solve the problem, or the clinic was free. We routinely had 12 or 15 horses. I remember one clinic with 25 horses. The clinics were four days long. I had to think on my feet. I had to be able to solve the problem, not to my satisfaction but to the owner's, and in such a way that it was not aggressive or abusive to the horse. When I put those parameters on my training, combined with the need to make the money to feed my family, it was important to develop techniques that would get the job done consistently. Those thousands of horses taught me the most.

That background gives me something that can't be duplicated by people who have trained just a few horses. It's true that they can do a lot of the same things that I do and teach, but when you are working a variety of horses, different things come up and you need experience. It took working a lot of horses to develop and refine the techniques I use now.

The second way that I learned was from the people who came to the clinics — just ordinary people who had a special way they got something done or who would give me a suggestion about the way they approached a problem. Sometimes their suggestion would spark an idea, and I'd develop it from there. I've also had a chance to bump up against some great trainers from all different training disciplines.

John and Zip have done demonstrations all over the country. One of John's most frequent themes is communication through the reins.

PH: *You've said that your training keeps changing. In what way?*

JL: I have a constant drive to improve. After working enough horses, all of a sudden I see another or better way to do something.

I am firmly convinced that there is always a better way to do things with a horse. I hear people say they learn from every horse, that they learn something every time they work a horse. I'm not that smart, evidently. I average 60-80 horses before I pick up one new idea. It takes a lot of exposure to a lot of horses for me to see something new, but then I'll see a little twist on one little thing. Then that mushrooms out into 10 other things. That's how and why my training keeps evolving, because of the exposure to the horses.

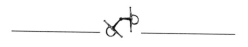

LYONISM ...

THE HORSE IS ALWAYS LEARNING SOMETHING, EITHER TO LISTEN TO ME OR NOT TO LISTEN TO ME. IF I PICK UP ON THE REIN AND THE HORSE DOES NOT STOP, THEN I HAVE TAUGHT HIM NOT TO PAY ATTENTION TO THE REIN.

People come to the clinics who have been to a clinic the year before and find it's completely different from last year, and that's the way it should be. If a trainer is doing the same thing for 10 years, then he hasn't improved in those 10 years. He has one years experience 10 times, not 10 years experience. We should all be continuing to learn and find better ways, so I constantly look for the better way.

That doesn't mean that the earlier way doesn't work. It worked just fine then and would work just as well now. The training principles don't change, but we work to find better training techniques.

PH: *Can you give us some examples of how things have changed from your early training days?*

JL: Well, for one thing, I've become increasingly specific. I find that when people are in trouble with their horses, when their horses are about to buck or run off, the people are trying to ride the whole horse. What they need to do is get control of one part of the horse. The secret of getting control — and eventually upper-level control of the whole horse — is gaining better control of the individual parts of the horse.

Going hand-in-hand with this is that I do a lot more ground work with the horse before I even put a halter on him than I used to. For instance, I'll do lots of leading lessons and inside and outside turns.

I've refined a lot of what I did in the round pen. I've always believed that you have to break a goal down into little parts, but I've found that the smaller the "baby steps," the more secure the progress you'll make. Developing all those baby steps has allowed my training to be more specific, and I end up with a better trained horse.

PH: *Was there a time in working with the horses that you really got scared or lost your nerve?*

JL: I've been scared, but I haven't lost my nerve. I've worked some really dangerous horses. I've learned that people who aren't afraid around horses are dangerous people. They are dangerous not only to themselves, but they are dangerous to their horses and to other people. Lack of fear is lack of knowledge. Horses are dangerous animals, whether we think they are or not.

The first rule of my training is that I shouldn't do anything that could get me hurt. I try to do everything as safely as I can. I think our own approach to safety is extremely important, not getting into a macho contest by saying, "By golly, I can break any horse; I'm tougher than any horse."

The most important reason that I haven't gotten hurt any worse than I have around horses is simply because God has watched over me. I truly believe that. I've worked too many dangerous horses and been in too many situations where I should have been hurt badly, but I haven't been. It's not because I'm any more brilliant or have special skills. Susie says I have two guardian angels who are constantly in front of God asking for reassignment. They are all dirty, their wings tattered and bent from holding horses up off of me and keeping horses from kicking me.

PH: *What is the biggest mistake you see people make when working with their horses?*

JL: It would be hard to determine the biggest, but one of the most prevalent is thinking that because you can ride the horse, he's broke. People get into all sorts of wrecks because the horse just isn't trained.

People are showing horses that they have trouble controlling when the environment isn't just perfect. Horses should be trained in the basic controls — give to pressure, leading lessons and so forth — so well that they can respond despite distractions.

Another mistake is thinking that equipment trains the horse. Bits, lunge lines, round pens and tie-downs don't train horses. People train horses. It's more important to understand training principles and to apply them in a consistent way than to own any equipment, including a round pen.

PH: *What would you recommend to someone who is struggling with a problem with their horse?*

JL: That everything you have heard about horse training is more complicated than it needs to be. Learn about the horse, treat him like a partner, and break your goal down into lots of baby steps. Find someplace to start — wherever you can ask the horse to do something and have him do it 100 percent of the time. ■ PH

28

Lyons, Another Perspective

When you have been trying to learn or understand something new, have you ever wished for a mouse in the corner to offer observations of how other folks have traveled the same path?

At *John Lyons' Perfect Horse* magazine, we receive lots of letters asking about how to better understand John's training, or asking about other readers' experiences as they integrate John's training into their situations. Our executive editor, Maureen Gallatin, has observed John teaching and has spoken with hundreds of clinic observers, symposium attendees, certification students and *Perfect Horse* readers about their experiences.

Perfect Horse: *Tell us what you've noticed in listening to* Perfect Horse *readers or observing people who attend John's clinics and symposiums?*

Maureen Gallatin: People approach John's training process with two primary objectives. The first group starts out looking for a fix for something they think of as broken. They want their horse to stop doing something — like running away, bucking, biting, rearing and so forth and they presume life will be perfect when "bad" behavior ends. So they want a simple recipe: They do this, and the horse does that. John's training provides, a solution for their control problems, and for some people, that's enough. You can do what John tells you to do and effectively correct undesirable behavior.

But even when most people "fix" something, they generally don't have the performance they want. Getting better performance or a better relationship is the second perspective.

The real value of John's teaching, as I've seen it played out, comes when people learn the training principles and can then apply them to their own goals and their own horse's situation. Then they are not dependent upon a "recipe" to train with. But getting to that stage takes a mindset change.

PH: *So, how does this change in thinking come about?*

MG: I've overheard lots of conversations that go something like the following one. The problem may vary — my horse goes too fast, doesn't steer, bites, drags me off at the end of a lead rope, etc. — but the path of thinking is usually the same.

Rider: John, I have a problem with my horse eating grass when we ride.
John: What do you want your horse to be doing?
Rider: Not eating grass.
John: But what do you want your horse to be doing instead of eating grass?
Rider: Walking forward, not eating grass.
John: At what speed?
Rider: At an energetic walk, but not rushing along — and not diving for grass.

If a horse has good ground manners, he is more likely to be respectful when ridden. Investing time in ground work pays off.

John: What do you want his head position to be like?

Rider: At a relaxed elevation, about even with his withers. And, I'd like him to be listening for my rein cues, instead of focusing on that grass!

John: When you are out trail riding, do you practice rein cues?

Rider: Not really. We just walk along, pretty relaxed until my horse dives for the grass.

John: So you want your horse to be listening for and obeying rein cues that you don't practice, even though he doesn't have anything else to do except think about the grass.

Rider: Well, I guess so. But he should know better.

John: When did you teach him to know better?

Rider: Well, I guess I just expected him to because I punish him for eating grass.

... And on it goes.

Initially, the rider's focus was the grass — just like her horse's. She really believed if she "corrected" the horse for eating grass, that he'd listen to her rein cues. But she hadn't practiced any cues, and she hadn't planned to practice any. Before this rider can improve her horse's performance substantially, she has to modify her thinking.

PH: *How do people start thinking beyond the quick-fix mentality?*

MG: Let me give you an example. John says, "Ride where you can, not where you can't." And he encourages students/readers to ask themselves "which would be easiest" questions. So if you know your horse has a tendency to put his head down to snatch at grass and your goal is to keep him moving, John's methods would encourage you to ask yourself, "Would it be easier to teach my horse to listen to my reins in a grassy pasture or a sand arena?" The answer is obvious, but folks have to know to ask the question in the first place.

Once the foundation for this kind of thinking is laid, the rider reports that he becomes increasingly confident and the horse seems to learn much faster than through the crisis-management system. Breaking a goal down into lesson plans with lots of steps allows the training to progress faster (even though it seems like more steps would take longer), and it allows the riders to become less reactive horsemen.

PH: *What do you mean by reactive?*

MG: John describes two kinds of horsemen — active and reactive. An active rider thinks ahead of the horse and makes decisions before

John doesn't try to outmuscle this horse. He's focused on control-
ling just one spot — the left shoulder.

there's a crisis. When the horse does something unexpected, the rider doesn't scold him but sticks to the original game plan, continuing to ask the horse for whatever the rider wanted before the distraction occurred. The active horseman isn't easily distracted, and, because his own "performance" is consistent, the horse settles down and becomes consistent. Eventually, even easily distracted horses become solid, because the rider has learned to focus on one thing — to really concentrate.

The opposite of an active rider is a reactive one, someone who reacts to everything the horse does. The horse steps left, and the rider makes a big deal about it. The horse raises his head as if he's about to spook, and the rider hollers at him or jerks on the reins, or worse yet, looks around to see what the horse is nervous about. (The active rider would think, "My horse's head is up and he's getting excited, so I'd better give him the 'calm down' cue.")

The reactive rider is always blaming somebody else for his horse's poor performance — the person who let her dog out of her car, or the fact there wasn't time to practice this week, or the other riders who shouldn't have cantered their horses, or even the "stupid" horse himself. The reactive rider not only reacts to everything the horse does, but he's also easily distracted by everything in his environment. Because "somebody" is always at fault, that person spends a lot of effort scolding his horse. He majors in "don't" cues — don't raise your head, don't canter, don't speed up. (Remember, the active rider would tell his horse to calm down. The reactive one scolds him for getting excited, and often has to resort to equipment, like a tie-down, to further prevent the horse from doing something bad.)

The reactive rider is always on the verge of being out of control, and he's rightly fearful of being out of control. And on it goes. While technique is important (telling the horse what to do rather than what not to do), it's really the person's mind set that makes the difference between being active or reactive. Again, you can either fight fires or prevent them.

PH: *What other changes in thinking help people better use John's training methods?*

MG: As I've watched — particularly people at the clinics working with their horses — a light bulb seems to come on in their heads when they realize they don't have to make the whole horse do something, like stop. When they concentrate on controlling one part of the horse and telling that one part specifically what to do, (i.e., left front foot move back), suddenly the whole horse comes under control without a fight.

Once people begin thinking about how to control one part of the horse, it doesn't really matter what part. Eventually the whole horse becomes controlled (though there are some parts that are easier to control or that more effectively control the whole horse).

So, for instance, the person who has a horse with poor leading manners, who bumps into the handler when he's being led, has a variety of ways to control that problem and improve the horse's leading manners, without getting into a fight with the horse. One low-threat way would be to put tension on the lead rope, pulling toward the horse's left shoulder. When the horse moves his left front foot back, or to the right, release the rope. When the horse becomes conditioned to that cue, and conditioned so well that he can respond even when he's excited, the person can apply it when he feels the horse begin to invade his space. That lead-rope cue will tell the horse to move his left foot away, and the person won't have to deal with the whole horse banging into them.

Or, if they have a horse who rears, they don't have to figure out how to make the horse stop rearing. They can teach the horse to drop the tip of his ear on cue; then, whenever he's thinking about rearing, they tell him to drop his ear. They aren't focused on the horse rearing, and he can't rear if his ear is only three feet from the ground.

The same thing applies to trailer loading. When people focus just on getting the horse in the trailer, they often get in a fight, or find out that other problems develop — like getting him out of the trailer or him jumping into the manger. If they concentrate on teaching each foot to load and unload, pretty soon the whole horse knows how to load and unload calmly.

Another mindset change is establishing an "agreement" with the horse about how the lesson will run. Rather than looking at each training project as a separate problem, if you look at it as just a new sentence in an established language, then each new lesson becomes fun — and it's tons less frustrating.

PH: *What do you mean by a language?*

MG: The key behind everything John does is establishing a cue or signal and making sure that cue means the same to the horse as to John. Just as the word "water" was a breakthrough for Helen Keller, when the horse learns that he gets a release when he does what John wants, the cue becomes a foundation word in his language.

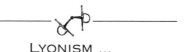

LYONISM ...

FEAR IS JUST COMMON SENSE IN DISGUISE. IT'S OK TO BE AFRAID AROUND HORSES. PEOPLE WHO AREN'T AFRAID AROUND HORSES CAN GET KILLED.

So John puts pressure on the horse in some way — body language, rein tension, toss of the lariat — and the horse learns that cue, or pressure, means John wants him to do something. By repetition, the horse learns that John is not going to hurt him and that John will use only enough pressure to stimulate a response from the horse. John will keep applying the pressure until the horse responds, then he lets up the pressure momentarily to let the horse know he's on the right track. Pressure only motivates the horse to change something; it doesn't tell the horse what change John wants.

The horse then experiments to find out what John wants. He's likely to make wrong guesses before he makes correct ones. John doesn't punish the horse for giving the wrong answer — that would be, in effect, punishing the horse for trying to do the right thing — but he keeps focus on what he wants. Sort of, "No, not that, but this." The lack of total release — and the fact that John is continuing to ask something of the horse — tells the horse that he should guess again, but it doesn't leave him afraid to guess again. The horse learns that the moment he gets the "right answer," the pressure is immediately released. It becomes a game.

Once you've established a foundation word — or actually a sequence of request-response-release, as I see it — then it doesn't really matter what the pressure is; the horse looks to find the answer you want. Once you, the trainer, know that arrangement, you can blunder along, and as long as you are consistent — pressure when you want something and release when the horse guesses correctly — you'll eventually make progress. The horse may not guess the right answer right off, but if he knows that you'll be fair with him and release when he gets it right, he'll begin experimenting.

PH: *Similar to the way someone in a foreign country tries to communicate in an unfamiliar language?*

MG: Exactly. It's like playing charades. When you know what a few gestures or movements mean, you can guess a whole lot more. The more right guesses you make, the more movements you learn. The horse is the guesser and you are the actor. Request — response — release. The smaller the request, the easier it is to get a right response, the quicker the horse gets rewarded, and the more fun the game is for both horse and trainer.

On the other hand, if the request is too hard, which usually means that the trainer should have broken the lesson down into more easy steps, the trainer ends up telling the horse, "No, not that. No, not that. No, not that." The horse can easily end up discouraged.

PH: *People are always asking John what cue they should use. What do you observe?*

MG: Just as you might use any number of methods to get your child's attention to tell him you want him to do something — a look, calling his name, clearing your throat, a hand signal — when the horse feels pressure, he knows that John wants something. That pressure may be a cue or may be actually a pre-cue. For instance, John kisses to the horse, then he signals what he wants. So if John wanted the horse's shoulders to move away from him in the round pen, his raising the lariat says, "Look at me," and his leaning toward the horse's shoulder with his body might be the cue that tells him "move your shoulders away." A human equivalent might be a mom who calls her child's name. He looks to her, then she asks him to take his plate to the sink.

Once that child looked to his mom, she could use any signal that he'd recognize as the cue to take his plate to the sink — words, a nod, pointing — or if he already knew the pattern, he might just look to her, then know he was excused from the table but he had to take his plate to the sink.

John says it doesn't really matter what cue you use. This often confuses people, but once they get it, a whole new world opens up to them. People trying to train their own horses are often so afraid of making a mistake that they feel locked into a having to get the cue right. But John says to just be yourself. Just tell the horse to do something with body language or a rein cue that seems natural to you. The horse doesn't instinctively know one from the other. You're going to take the time to teach the cue to the horse, and when you really need your horse to respond in a tight situation, you're going to do what comes naturally to you.

So you may as well develop a cue that works for you. The keys are to use it consistently and for it not to hurt the horse. So you wouldn't want to hit the horse with the lariat, if you could point instead. You don't want the cue to be an irritation. Instead, it's like a password, like your PIN number at the ATM. The bank doesn't care what four digits you choose, but since you use those numbers every time, they should be easy to remember.

PH: *Are there other areas where people's thinking gets them off track in working with their horses?*

MG: A big one is trust. John says most people confuse affection with trust. They think their horse trusts them if he is friendly or allows himself to be petted or saddled. That's trust to a certain extent, but he may not trust them enough to hang around without a halter when the vet comes to give shots. When a horse doesn't obey, it's not a betrayal of trust — a personal failure — it's just evidence of a lack of training. Without some measure of training, trust isn't a factor in the discussion. It's different than how we think of trust with people.

Trust is actually a byproduct of control. When the horse learns that you can control him without causing him pain, then he begins to trust your leadership. When he just comes smooching around, he's the one in control, so he's merely trusting himself and his ability to get away if he has to. He's not really trusting you. But, when he responds to your cue to "come," he's exhibiting trust. Or when his instincts urge him to run after the other horses, but instead he obeys your rein cue to stop, he's telling you that he trusts you.

PH: *In a nutshell, what advice would a "mouse in the corner" have for our* Perfect Horse *readers?*

MG: That all this isn't as hard as it may seem at first. It's common-sense stuff. Listen to what John teaches not as if he's the great horseman (though he is). Listen as if he's a wise friend who has confidence in you coaching you along. Think active — not reactive. Forget about scolding your horse (or yourself), but concentrate on developing a lesson plan.

Ask yourself if you've really developed a foundation word, or if it may seem to your horse as if your signals come out of nowhere.

When you run into a snag, ask yourself what cue you wish the horse was responding to. You may discover you've been telling him "don't," but not telling him what you want.

And then, what John says all the time, "Accept improvement." If you make little strides forward, you'll eventually get to your goal. If today your horse turned or stopped a little better than yesterday, that's improvement. Don't chew on him about the other things that didn't improve. Keep it positive, and keep it fun. ▣

196 ■ THE MAKING OF A PERFECT HORSE

Notes

29

Lyons I Have Known

This story is fictional.
Any resemblance to persons (or ornery horses)
with whom you are familiar is purely coincidental.

In the past few years, I (Zip) have begun to realize that my life has been a bit more adventurous than that of other horses. I've traveled to almost every state, taught manners to hundreds of untrained horses and made thousands of people aware of what a horse is capable of learning. I have made friends across the nation and have even had my likeness made into a Stone model horse. These things have happened because of my work with a certain nationally known horse trainer (who insists that horses can't tell stories).

My early years were spent on a Colorado ranch. I worked cattle, helped with ranch chores and survived more disasters than most horses could ever imagine. Through it all, the one person who has always been there, getting me into these crazy situations, and thankfully having the resourcefulness to get me out of them, has been my friend, John Lyons.

John and I have a special sort of relationship that is not so easy to explain. There is love, pride and mutual respect, which has made it possible for us to work together as a team for over 20 years.

But, there is another element to our relationship — whenever we can, we drive the other one crazy. We take turns. And although other people may not realize it, it is this element that makes us different, makes us special, makes us a perfect team and makes working together fun. Because, when you're concentrating on the little annoyances of life, you find out that the big ones have worked themselves out without needing to be worried over. We learned the

Unfortunately, Dream (above) died in a trailer accident, so we couldn't verify the story ... and Zip's sworn to silence.

best way to do things by trying the worst ways first. We see who is going to teach the other one about life.

However, I gotta admit, I'm not the only horse John has ever driven nuts while trying out a well-meant but half-baked idea. One day, John learned a lesson of his own with a dear old stablemate of mine, Dream, a big, muscular Quarter Horse stallion.

Lessons learned and unlearned

Ranch work is never easy, roaming for miles across pastureland, catching calves that don't want to be caught and generally lending a hand to whatever comes along. But, on this particular day, I was lucky — John decided to take Dream, giving me the day off.

I didn't expect John and Dream to be back before dark, so I was surprised to see them return in the early afternoon. With one look at the pair, I knew something was amiss. Dream was walking kind of funny, not really lame but not quite right either. John was muttering to himself.

As they entered the barn, I followed them, wondering what had happened. John seemed thoroughly disgusted as he gathered up medical supplies. I looked at John and Dream. Neither of them was hurt, so what was going on? John untacked Dream, still muttering and occasionally shaking his head. Then he left.

By this time my curiosity was pretty strong, so I turned my attention to Dream. I just had to ask, "Hey, Dream, why are you home so early today?"

Dream gave me one of those "Oh, you wouldn't believe it if I told you" kind of looks. I urged, "You can't come in here walking all sore and have John leave in disgust without expecting to tell me all the details!"

Dream shook himself all over, then turned to me. "You know, somedays I think John is just plain crazy. You wouldn't believe what he did today." Well, I'd known John a whole lot longer than Dream had, so I'd believe just about anything.

"We were working up on the north slope," Dream began, "roping calves for John to doctor. You know how I hate doing that kind of stuff. It gets so boring just standing there waiting for John to get finished so we can go do the next one. He'd been shoving pills down the throats of calves all morning, and everything seemed to be going along fine. Then, John decided that he wanted to rope this big ol' steer.

"When John headed me at it, I looked back at him to see if he was sure he wanted to tackle something quite so large. I tell you, Zip, that steer weighed every bit as much as I do. But John's face told me we were going to catch that steer if it killed us. As the steer was moving along, John roped it, but I didn't understand why he roped it around its middle, instead of around the neck. 'Course, it didn't make any difference to me: I knew I could hold him no matter how John had him roped."

Well, I could think of several reasons, but I didn't want to interrupt his train of thought, so I just nodded.

Dream continued his tale. "I backed up hard, tightening the rope to hold the steer facing me. It had the lariat rope wrapped around its back, behind its shoulders, with the end leading to my saddle horn, where it was tied fast. John got down, but instead of approaching the steer, he went off to the side and sat down. I looked at him like he had lost his mind. Why am I standing out here holding this dumb steer if John doesn't want to do something with it?"

About this time, I began to figure out what was going on. I had heard John complaining that Dream was falling asleep on the job. You see, when roping calves, the horse should keep the rope tight between himself and the calf until the cowboy gets the calf down and sits on it. Then the horse should move up, slackening the pressure on the rope, so that the calf can swallow the medication. This is where it gets tricky for the horse, because you have to watch real close and take up the slack again if it looks like the cowboy is going to lose control of the calf.

I had warned Dream several times that when he and John were treating calves he needed to mind his business better, but he was a big, bold, arrogant fellow who didn't much listen to advice. I couldn't help but wonder if John had chosen today to teach Dream a lesson.

Dream paused long enough to grab a mouthful of hay. Chewing thoughtfully, he continued his tale. "So, I'm standing out in the middle of this field, facing off this steer, and John's just sitting in the shade. I didn't understand what was going on, but I know my business, so I just stood there, eyeballing that steer, which got boring. That ol' steer was just as confused as I was, so he wasn't going anywhere. I relaxed.

"In a little while, John got up and walked toward the steer. Naturally, the steer moved off, to get away from him. That caused the rope to pull suddenly on my saddle horn. It threw me off balance for a second, but I stepped sideways and took up the slack again. You know, Zip, what didn't make any sense at all was that me stopping that steer when it moved didn't seem to please John at all. Now I ask you, does that make any sense?" he asked as he headed back for another bite of hay.

Actually, it made a lot of sense. My hunch had been right. John had decided to teach Dream about napping on the job. You see, whenever Dream talks about just standing there, what he's really doing, but won't admit it, is sleeping. That really gets John's goat. I figure John used an old roper's trick to show Dream what can happen if he takes his eyes off that rope.

The idea is that if the horse isn't paying attention, the steer can run off, snatching the slack out of the rope quickly enough to knock the horse off balance. That's what John had meant to happen to Dream when he started walking toward the steer. The only thing he forgot was that Dream was built like a Sherman tank.

I can imagine how aggravated John was when Dream just sidestepped and continued to hold the steer. Dream had definitely won that round, showing that he didn't need to be awake to handle whatever might come along. 'Course, Dream didn't even realize he'd been challenged, much less won a battle. It's always the same with these big, beautiful ones, plenty of muscle but not much between the ears.

Continuing the story

Anyway, I didn't intend to explain all this to Dream, so I just sighed sympathetically and asked what happened next.

Dream shook his head in remembered aggravation. "When I was

facing off the steer again with the rope taut, John stood there for a few minutes. Then he started walking toward the steer again. Well, this time the steer didn't charge off, it began to walk in a semicircle around me. When it got behind me, the rope bumped against my ankles.

"Zip, you know how I hate to have things close to my feet, so I stepped over the rope with my forefoot and then with my hind foot. I thought for sure the steer would keep on circling, so I would just step over the rope with my other two feet when it came to them. Guess that's what I get for thinking! Looking back, that wasn't the smartest thing I've ever done.

"I'm standing there, the rope is tied to my saddle horn, passing between my front legs and between my back legs, and this steer decides to leave in a hurry. The rope went taut, slapping me in places no stallion ever tolerates."

By now, I'm reaching for a big mouthful of hay myself — anything to keep from bursting out laughing. I know poor old Dream was hurting, but the whole picture was just too funny. I managed to ask, without giggling, "What did you do?"

Dream snorted. "What do you think I did? I left! I had had enough. The steer was still tied to my saddle horn, so he didn't have any choice but to come along. 'Course, cattle are so slow, that after about two strides, he fell down. I didn't let that stop me. I was putting as much distance between me and John Lyons as I could.

"I ran a ways up a mountain before I decided to stop, turn around and look. John was just a small figure in the distance, but I could see him starting to follow my trail, shaking his head as he walked. I must say, when I turned my attention to the steer, I did feel guilty, seeing the rope burns and the bruises from being dragged a bit. That's why John was gathering up those medical supplies. I imagine he's going to be spending the rest of the afternoon treating cuts and bruises."

By this time, fatigue set in, and Dream settled in his stall for a good, long nap. I continued to eat my hay, laughing softly to myself at the thought of that big ox of a horse dragging that steer off right under John's nose.

In the never-ending game of who is training who, I think Dream won this round. Funny, though, when you think of it. Somehow, trying to teach a lesson never seems to work out quite as planned. ▣

by Bright Zip as told to Kay Whittington.

Notes

30

Helpful Info

Every sport and training method has its own lingo. We've compiled some of the more common terms used in "Lyonizing" your horses.

Cue: A signal that you specifically teach to your horse to indicate a specific behavior you want him to do. A cue is like a password — something that both you and the horse recognize, but may have no value on its own. The cue is never the reason a horse does a behavior. It merely signals the behavior you are requesting.

Cues may be physical, such as putting tension on a rein. They may be voice cues, such as saying "Whoa," or they may be body language cues, such as moving toward a horse's nose to indicate that you want him to turn away from you.

Give to the bit: This is an exercise in which the rider takes all the slack out of a rein while thinking about the horse moving a particular part of his body, say, his nose or his left front foot. When the horse does move that part of the body in the direction the rider requested, we refer to that movement — that act of obedience — as "giving" to the request. The rider should then release the rein, rewarding the horse and indicating that the horse did the right thing.

The first exercise in "giving to the bit" lessons is often referred to as the **baby give.** In this, the rider requests that the horse move his nose energetically to the side where there is tension on the rein, as if the horse were going to look at the rider's knee. The "give" could be movement of one-quarter of an inch or up to several inches. The important part is not the extent of the movement but the eagerness with which the horse responds.

The "baby give" is the basic word in a "giving to the bit" language. Once the horse learns the baby give, he also learns the concept that slack taken out of one rein means that he should move part of his body. When he moves the part of the body the rider was requesting be moved, the rider releases the rein.

A horse can "give" to the bit with any part of his body. When he gives with his hip, for instance, we sometimes say the "rein is connected to the hip." The rider will use what appears to be the same cue to ask for various movements, but with practice, the horse can differentiate between requests for, say, his head to drop or his right front foot to move right.

Calm down cue: This is basically "giving to the bit" with a downward movement of the horse's head. When the lesson is done fully, the instinct for the horse to raise his head when he feels pressure on the bit is replaced with a conditioned response to drop the head. When the horse drops his head, he calms down.

Replacement concept: When a horse is doing something you don't want him to do, replace that behavior with behavior that you want. For instance, if a horse is being too mouthy, chewing on a lead rope, for instance, practice leading lessons

Yield to pressure: Similar to the "give to the bit" concept, the horse learns that when he feels pressure, for example, a pull on the lead rope, he should move toward the source of pressure, rather than resist it, which would be the natural, untrained reaction.

WESN lesson: This is a directional-control lesson done with the horse on a halter and lead. It teaches the horse to move left (west), right (east), back (south) and forward (north) on cue. It is particularly helpful for horses who have a tendency to invade the handler's space or not be respectful of halter cues.

Sacking out: This term refers to the process of exposing a horse to an object that scares him — like a saddlepad — but in a low-threat way, and removing the threat before the horse feels he has to move. The horse then learns to control his emotions.

Spook in place: This is a lesson to develop emotional control in a horse, in which the horse learns to replace his instinct to run away from danger with a conditioned response to turn to face the noise or object that scares him.

The *John Lyons' Perfect Horse* Library contains detailed lessons for solving the most common training problems. Below we've listed the problem or lesson and the book where you'll find the solution. The complete series, of which this is Volume 8, addresses training, care, feeding, horsekeeping and veterinary matters.

Volume 1 — Communicating with Cues, Part I
Cues; Developing lesson plans; Learning cycles
Biting; Headshyness; Bridling
Pulling back; Yield to Pressure
Picking up hooves
"Go forward" cue; Lunge line training; WESN lesson
Speed control (riding); Active and reactive riders
Buddy sour (emotional control)
"Calm down" cue
Teach horse to lie down

Volume 2 — Communicating with Cues, Part II
Round pen work, including saddling and first ride
Sacking out
Spook in place
Rear-ending lesson (from the ground and saddle)
"Don't shy" cue
Getting a horse's attention
Snaffle bit advice
Trail riding advice
Trailer loading

Volume 3 — Veterinary Care for the Perfect Horse
Vaccinations; Deworming; Coggins testing; Rabies
Arthritis; Colic; EPM; HYPP; Tying up
Eye problems; Blindness; Strangles
Chronic Respiratory problems; Thyroid

Volume 4 — Communicating with Cues, Part III
Working with foals
"Giving to the bit" lessons; Head toss problems
Kicking on the trail; Cinchy problems
Evaluating a clinic (trainer)
Catching the horse; Headshy story

Volume 5 — Raising and Feeding the Perfect Horse
Feeding myths: Buying good hay; Alfalfa; Grains
Bran; Beet pulp; Soy; Protein
B vitamins; Electrolytes: Antioxidants; Supplements for hooves
Problem broodmares; Orphan foal
Guide to foaling; Metabolic bone disease

Volume 6 — Perfectly Practical Advice About Horsemanship
Yield to Pressure (foal training)
Living with horses; Body language; Herd dynamics
Riding on the road (lessons and advice)
Preventing bucking
Riding in the rain
Staying safe; What to do when a rider falls

Volume 7 — Horsekeeping: Expert Advice About Tack and Barn
Buying horse property; House-barn combinations
Fire prevention; Covered arena options; Ventilation
Electric fencing; Vinyl fencing
Manure spreaders; Trailer hitches
Saddle lingo; Saddle fit

The Making of a Perfect Horse series is available from
Belvoir Publications, Inc.
800-424-7887/203-661-6111
www.perfecthorse.com

Index

For information regarding the monthly magazine,
John Lyons' Perfect Horse, or other books in the *John Lyons Perfect Horse Library,* see our web site www.perfecthorse.com or call the publisher, Belvoir Publications, Inc. at 800-424-7887.

EXECUTIVE EDITOR: MAUREEN GALLATIN
ASSISTANT EDITORS: CINDY FOLEY AND LIZ NUTTER
CONTRIBUTING WRITERS: SUE SUSHIL, DULAI WENHOLZ, KAY WHITTINGTON
VETERINARY EDITOR: ELEANOR KELLON VMD
BOOK DESIGN AND LAYOUT: SUSAN R. TOMKIN
PHOTO CREDITS: MAUREEN GALLATIN, CHARLES HILTON, MARK WALPIN